Riska

Memories of a Dayak Girlhood

RISKA OPRA SARI

Edited by Linda Spalding

With an Afterword by Carol J. Pierce Colfer

THE UNIVERSITY OF GEORGIA PRESS
Athens

Paperback edition published in 2000
in the United States of America by
the University of Georgia Press
Athens, Georgia 30602

Published by arrangement with Alfred A. Knopf Canada, a division
of Random House of Canada Limited, Toronto, Canada.

Printed in the United States of America
04 03 02 01 00 P 5 4 3 2 I

Library of Congress Cataloging-in-Publication Data
available upon request

ISBN 0-8203-2270-9

Riska

For my beloved daughter,
Karina Hagafiona Monica

I would like to thank all the people at Knopf Canada who helped make this book a reality. My special gratitude to Linda Spalding, who helped and inspired me. Thank you, Linda, for all your help and endless encouragement. My gratitude to Quentin Van Soldt for all his support and patience along the way. I thank Mr. H. B. Collett from Alam Sari Resort, Bali, for his encouragement and support. I thank Ms. Carol Colfer for her support. My hope is that with this book, people will recognize our existence, our tribal land, our problems with the destroyed forest on which our whole life depends.

— Riska Orpa Sari

Contents

Introduction

A BROWN RIVER, shallow enough to ford. Long iron-wood buildings, bowed roofs and overarching trees. This is what I remember of a place that now seems to me to be suspended between earth and sky with, sometimes, a figure standing in between, perhaps in the river, washing her long hair and wrapped in batik.

When I am not remembering the Delang River and Riska standing in it — a vision that is a blur of various mornings and afternoons, of other faces and bodies, of children, silence, laughter — I remember three events that changed my view of her life. They involved soldiers, a picnic and a ceremony. In reverse order.

Riska was born in Kudangan, a Dayak village in the heart of Borneo that we visited together in May of 1997. It sits at the top of the Lamandau River system, which originates high in the Schwaner Mountains on the border between West and Central Kalimantan and flows straight south to the Java Sea. The village must once have been wondrously remote, since the upstream areas of the Lamandau are nearly inaccessible, even by boat. But now there is a timber road. And things are different.

We'd made the long, difficult trip with a rented car and driver up the rutted gouge through the forest all the way from Pangkalan Bun on the southern coast of Kalimantan, the Indonesian part of Borneo. We were surrounded by tribespeople who maintain most of the customs of their ancestors, but whose traditional way of life is challenged by transmigration from other islands, which is promoted by the Indonesian government. In the past ten or fifteen years half a million settlers have moved to Kalimantan with incentives of cleared land and a year's worth of seed. When they realize that the shallow soil will not support them, they go to work as labourers on the palm-oil plantations that have replaced the primeval forest. Palm oil is big business in Indonesia, and even the Dayaks, pushed into a cash economy, are beginning to take work on plantations or with the timber companies who have cut down half of Borneo's great rain forest and are trying to cut down the rest.

I'd read enough books to know that these "headhunters of Borneo" have a fascinating history, excel in certain arts and make the best blowguns in the world, but the taking of heads is illegal now, and when thousands of Madurese settlers in West Kalimantan were slaughtered by Dayaks in February and March of 1997, the news was entirely suppressed. Neither Riska nor I heard anything about it.

During our visit to Kudangan, I listened continually to Riska, whose nearly simultaneous translation of whatever was happening around us had become routine over the many weeks we had been together. But the whispered words that I noticed being exchanged in some corners were never repeated to me. When a room became suddenly tense, Riska seemed to fall silent. What were they saying? "I can't talk," Riska said, by way of explanation. Later she said, "There is going to be a ceremony to protect the village."

The ceremony was going to be private, attended by only a few of the village men. But the Mantir Adat (the chief of law) of Sekombulan village was coming downriver and since he was a vivid part of Riska's childhood memories, we thought we would try to catch a glimpse of him.

It was a short walk from the house of Riska's uncle, where we were staying, along a gnarled path between weather- and time-worn longhouses and through overhanging, large-leaved trees. We seemed to be entering a more textured zone. After negotiating the path, keeping our eyes fastened on the ground, we were surprised when someone spoke to us from a doorway high above. We hesitated, then climbed a notched pole that led to a first porch, where we left our sandals, and a second pole that led to a doorway adorned with a finely carved dragon. "They are inviting us," Riska explained in her quiet voice as she stooped to enter the dark interior and drew in her breath. Above, on rafters that spanned the width of this old ironwood longhouse were row upon row of the huge antique Chinese jars the Dayaks have given and traded and treasured for centuries. They were barely discernible in the dark.

Once, there might have been human heads up there as well, but these days they must be secreted away like the relics required for this ceremony, ancient pieces of bone and stone that most of the men in the longhouse had not seen before that afternoon. The Dayak living along the upper reaches of Kalimantan's great rivers have a strong sense of tradition which has actually been reinforced by Dutch colonials and Protestant missionaries, whose motive was to keep Islam out of Kalimantan's interior. Christianity is the prevailing religion of the interior now, but a sizable minority of Dayaks still adhere to the religion of their ancestors, which is called Kaharingan.

So it was that when the carved dragon door was closed behind us, Riska and I saw the Mantir Adat of Sekombulan and a small group of men sitting on the floor in the shadows behind a screen of smoke and incense examining a dish that contained the various relics — the fozzilised antler of a deer, some stones, some shells. "Very rare," Riska murmured. I could tell that she was moved. Twenty years earlier, at the age of eight, she had left Kudangan in a longboat to take up the marginal life of a Dayak living among Muslims on the coast. Because her mother had not been able to obtain release from her years of indentured obligation as a teacher in this village, the family had escaped at night, taking almost nothing so as not to arouse suspicion, and paddling for several days. Now Riska had come back. Perhaps for that reason, or because, as an outsider, I was presumed to be important, we were invited to watch the ceremony.

As a small chicken was being held over a bowl of raw rice, I assumed, based on a previous experience of this sort, that the chicken was not going to be sacrificed, but simply nicked so that her blood would anoint the rice, the Dayak's link to the spirit world. The old man was chanting. Riska was listening hard. And the thick rice wine called *tuak* that the Dayaks make and store in their ceramic jars was being poured and passed. What I remember about the next few minutes is smoke, blood, the cider-like taste of the wine, chanting, a bunch of men in shorts and T-shirts tense with formality. I remember being shocked that I was witness to such an event.

Three years previously I'd met Riska for the first time in the tiny airport at Pangkalan Bun, where she had lived with her parents since coming downriver. If that dangerous trip in a longboat had changed Riska's life irrevocably by taking her out of the traditional life of a Dayak tribeswoman and propelling her into a future of uncertain complexity, our meeting was perhaps as momentous. At work on a book about primatologist Birute Galdikas, I was travelling with my two daughters, anticipating ten days on the Sekonyer River in the national park of Tanjung Puting, where Galdikas had established a research station known as Camp Leakey in the early 70s. There, she spent years studying wild orang utans and working to rehabilitate orang utans who had been illegally captured.

My plan was to spend the ten days ahead of us on a riverboat, a *kelotok*, and we'd been warned that we would need to find a guide who would prevail first upon human authorities and then on the various forces of nature that would be ranged against us. So, even alighting, we had looked around, wondering how to go about finding such a person. Then, while we waited for our backpacks to come out of the belly of the plane, we were greeted by Riska, who announced that she was a guide, but who looked too diminutive, too shy and far too ladylike in her well-pressed blue dress to prevail upon anything, human or otherwise.

Two of our packs had not arrived but were still in the Semerang airport back on Java. Riska took it upon herself to have them sent to the hotel when the next plane arrived, and as she did so, I watched her calm assurance, her confident negotiations on our behalf, and began to wonder whether she might be free to accompany us.

"What do you do, exactly?" we asked, climbing into the taxi she'd managed to find in an empty parking lot and eyeing the blue dress, the black shoes, the hair tightly coiled in a bun.

"I am working for a travel bureau."

Good, I thought. But we were more hungry than curious and once we had registered ourselves at the hotel, Riska offered to take our passports to the local police for security clearance. "While we're waiting, do you want to go to our best restaurant?" she asked. And then with an infectious smile, "Or at least our most expensive one."

No doubt our friendship began with that tiny moment, when it seemed to me that she might be not only the guide we needed but also an interpreter, someone whose wit and perspective would make sense of what we were going to be seeing. Over lunch in the "most expensive" restaurant, which happened to be Chinese, I asked her if she would like to come upriver with us and, as we were not part of her agency's tour group, if she would be able to ask for some time off.

To both questions, she simply said "yes" and she framed the word with her irridescent smile, adding that she would check on our boat and pick up our passports on the way. I had no idea how she got around so easily, since the car had gone back to the airport and the boat she was checking on was in another town, but I didn't ask. She was twenty-five, the age of my youngest daughter, and by afternoon, when she came to our room with the passports, she was wearing her trekking gear — sandals, khaki pants and a long-sleeved shirt — and we never saw the blue dress again. From then on, her hair was braided or hanging straight past her waist, and she was pleasantly but forcefully in charge.

"Is the boat all right?" I asked.

"Oh, yes."

"And you can be our guide?"

With her second "yes," the enterprise — including my book — began taking shape in my mind. I saw us as four women who would be living on a riverboat in the heart of the rain forest. It was not what I had first imagined, but it was somehow more interesting. Riska would bring her experience, tact and humour to the process. She had made numerous trips to Camp Leakey, was immediately interested in the project, and eager to help. In our first few hours on the kelotok, she told us that there was no other female guide, no other Dayak guide in Kalimantan, the significance of which has to be seen in the context of both Muslim culture, where young women and men are seriously compromised by spending *any* time alone together, and Dayak culture, where the idea of going off into the rain forest for adventure is usually a male one. That this was the case became obvious to us only very slowly, as if the picture were gradually being revealed to us through an emulsion. Over the days we spent together, my daughters and I had to watch, listen, then wonder about what we were seeing and hearing. Riska explained many things, but she did not explain how unusual she was. She had not herself, I think, begun to understand her own life.

The Dayak are riverine, forest dwellers — people who use swidden or slash-and-burn techniques to cultivate vegetables, fruit and rice, hunting and gathering on the side. As our guide on that first trip, Riska taught us a great deal about the trees, birds and animals of the forest around us and a little about the beliefs of her people, who live in a nation and culture dominated by Muslim influence. "Do you eat pig?" she asked, when we told her we didn't eat meat. This question is simply asked to determine loyalties since pork, which is anathema to the Muslims, is a centre-piece of the Dayak diet.

Today, most of the Dayaks of the Lamandau River system have converted to Christianity (which allows the eating of pork), and their religious customs involve a mix of traditions. From their Austronesian origins — out of the Asian mainland via the Philippines five thousand years ago — come elaborate two-part funerals. The first part is performed soon after death with masked dancers, priests, drums and a great deal of formalized mourning. During the second funeral, or *tiwah*, the bones of the dead are exhumed, cleaned, placed in ceramic jars, then in painted and carved wooden ossuaries called *sandung*. This second funeral is a long, expensive process and families may wait years before collectively celebrating a tiwah. But it must be performed in order to ensure the soul its place in upper heaven and to keep the living safe from evil spirits.

Two thousand years ago, when they moved up the Malay penninsula and back to the mainland coast of southeast Asia, the Dayaks incorporated the bird of the upper world and the reptile of the underworld into their beliefs. Hornbills and crocodiles are now the primary symbols of Kaharingan belief, but other deities crossed the ocean with them on great outrigger canoes so long ago that they took root in Borneo's soil, and now Jesus and Mary Magdalene are planted there, too.

In Borneo, as settlements grew and sea trade with Asia increased, the Dayak began to forge metal tools and when those tools made it possible, they extracted starch from the sago palm and carved from the well-named ironwood the most efficient blowguns in the world. They began to domesticate the animals around them and to cut down trees and burn them to fertilize the otherwise poor soil. In the fields they cleared, called *ladangs*, they began to plant rice, a deity whose contentment makes possible a good harvest.

"Maybe it all started," Riska told us, "when some men of the Jarai River went to the forest to hunt wild boar. On the way they met a bunch of men from the Makaham River and killed all but one. They told him to go back and warn his people never to enter the area. But a few years later, when they heard that the men of the Makaham were coming up on a headhunting raid, they decided to move to a safer place themselves. They made a ceremony with an eagle as mediator and he flew off in the direction of the Kahayan River, so three hundred people left the village, bringing everything they could carry and burning the rest. All the longhouses, all the ladangs were burned. Together, they entered the dark, wet forest, crossing mountains and rivers no one had ever crossed before. All up and down the branches of the Kahayan they stopped, first one family and then another — many branches — guided by the eagle called Atung Sempung. In this way, they avoided the headhunters and established new homes."

I said, "That's how the Dayaks dispersed?"

"My mother's tribe," Riska said. "But I grew up on the Delang, and the story there is a little different, although it also has a bird, because their messages are very important to us."

She looked wistful. "I wish I could tell the real story of my people," she said. It was the last afternoon of that first trip, and we were in the Pangkalan Bun airport again, waiting to depart. I told her I thought the most interesting way to do it would be to tell the story of her own life.

"Oh no. That isn't interesting!" she said. "No one would be interested in that."

I suppose it was fortunate that our flight was two hours late and that she was kind enough to stay by our sides as we waited for the plane that was probably going to separate us for ever. The ten days of living together on a small river kelotok had been so charged for all of us that they might have been weeks. We four women knew each other intimately in terms of habits and character, but our life stories — "hers" and "ours"— were still worlds apart. On that particular level of communication, we had all been extremely discreet.

"How would I begin?" Riska wondered, as we sat in matching plastic chairs in the departure area with its three exits: one to the washroom, one to the prayer room and one to the hot tarmac.

I said, "Just keep a notebook, write things down. You'll find a way to write what you want to say, but you have to be part of it or it won't have real meaning."

She pulled a notebook out of her pack. "Like this?" and she was already opening it, pressing it flat, showing me the lovely, fluid handwriting that covered the first page. "Here I tell about the tiwah, that's our funeral. I'm writing . . ."

"In English!" I said. "Why are you doing that?"

She said, "So that you . . ." But the plane was suddenly announced. We could see it, hear it and feel it all at once as it lowered itself and lurched to a stop a few yards away.

"Maybe if I come back," I said vaguely, "I could read it," though it was unlikely that I would ever see her again. I was going back to Canada to write my own book. I could not imagine crossing the great gulf of water, air, culture and time in the near future, and possibly not ever again. We all hugged rather circumspectly and wished each other well. If it was hard to believe that the close community we had become was about to disintegrate, I was nevertheless moving on mentally to Jakarta, wondering where we would find a room for the night and how much of the capital of Indonesia we would have time to see in a brief twenty-four hours.

When I got back to Toronto, I received an occasional letter from Riska remembering the ten days we had spent as four women living and trekking together as "like a picnic, when I think back on it." Later she sent updates from her trips into the national park and her visits with the orang utans and I began to look forward to them. As my book progressed, it became apparent that my research was not finished. Then it seemed that I *would* be going back. To Borneo. To Kalimantan. This time, my days would have to be spent in a small cabin in the rain forest where I would learn more about orang utans and the rehabilitation of orang utan orphans. There would be no telephone, no electricity, no running water, no food except what I took in by boat, and I would be more or less stranded for three weeks without any form of transportation except my own legs. Even visits to the other stations in the park, like Camp Leakey, would be difficult. There would be no company during that time, except the orang utans themselves. I wrote to Riska and asked her if she would come with me. "And bring your notebook," I suggested, to be polite.

A month later, we established ourselves in a small cabin in the national park. There are no roads in that part of Borneo, and as I had expected, without a boat we were stuck in our stifling cabin for hours at a time — hours when we listened to the tapes we'd bought in Pangkalan Bun on my Walkman or sat by the table covered with most of our food and stared at each other and talked. The cabin was shut up — windows nailed tight, doors locked — to keep out invading orang utans who would have taken all of our food and wreaked havoc in no time. Because any opening, however screened, would have been an invitation, we didn't even have the pleasure of a breeze. The river was full of crocodiles and flesh-eating fish, so it was not safe to swim, and for several hours a day, it was far too hot to walk or even to go outside. What we had was the table and two red plastic chairs. I put the tape recorder on the table next to our potatoes and crackers and rice and we listened to Riska's two favourite tapes: John Denver and a rough imitation of Elvis.

It was while sitting on those chairs that Riska began to tell me about her mother's insistence that the family leave the village of Kudangan on the Delang River and make the seven-day journey by longboat to a town where her children could go to junior high school. It was there, during those impossible, hot hours, that I begged her to let me turn on the tape recorder while she talked.

"I don't know what to say," she began.

I said, "Just go on telling me about the village."

But as soon as she heard her own voice replayed, she became disgusted, said that her English was "ugly," that she sounded "stupid" and that, anyway, she had nothing interesting to talk about.

"But you want to tell the story of the Dayaks?"

"Not like this. No. On paper."

"I think that would probably take years."

She went to her room and came back with the notebook. The same one she'd shown me a year before. "It's almost full," she said.

Riska's handwriting is beautiful and her written English, which she was still using for her notes, was more graceful than her spoken words. I was surprised. "Oh, we are taught to write," she said, waving her hand. The cultural notes she had made were amazingly detailed. I couldn't imagine describing anything from my own childhood that accurately.

English was, I found out, Riska's third or even fourth language. At home, they spoke her mother's dialect; in the village, they spoke her father's. She hadn't learned Indonesian until she went to school. English had been learned in a short course, over a period of weeks, and was otherwise self-taught. "And I'm going to study Japanese," she told me. "Some day I want to go to Bali, where they teach German and Japanese."

I said, "But still, this isn't your first language. It's complicated to explain but you use English words that may not mean what you think they mean. . . . You say jungle, for example, but I would call this a forest."

"Jungle, *utan*. Forest, *rimba*." She smiled. "I know the difference."

"If we could combine some of this with your own story . . ."

She shook her head.

"Okay," I agreed. "Nothing personal, but let's add some detail." With the tape recorder experimentally turned on, we began discussing the first notes she had made, beginning with the tiwah, Riska describing the various stages of the ceremonies and the meanings attached to certain practices. When I asked her questions, she answered, then listened to the recording to see if she sounded "stupid." Several times she snapped it off, especially when I interjected, asking her something she didn't care to answer. Finally, on the verge of tears, she announced dismally that she was going to her room to "have a sleep."

This room had provided one of the main incentives for the trip as far as Riska was concerned, for she lived in a house where she had no private corner to call her own. In addition to our two rooms, each with two narrow beds and a plastic night table, there was a tiny room with a kerosene stove on the floor and a central room with the table on which sat our foodstuffs, our tapes, books and the tiny but ominous tape recorder. In the far corner, beyond the "kitchen," was the *mandi* with its squat toilet and several pails of river water which, though cool, was laced with toxins, both organic and inorganic (it was highly acidic and full of mercury from the illegal gold mining going on upriver).

As Riska went off to her room, I felt stranded and confused. "Take the tape recorder in with you," I suggested. "See if it's easier to talk when I'm not there."

She said, "You might not like the real me," and the silence that followed was more oppressive than the terrible heat of the late afternoon. I wondered why I was pushing Riska to do something she apparently had so little taste for. I didn't know how we could possibly spend three weeks alone in this place or how we would even get through the rest of the day. I had tried to explain it to myself: her life was fascinating, especially as it had changed so radically and because she was in a position to describe that change.

It crossed my mind that my enthusiasm for the project had something to do with feeling out of control. In our cabin, I was helpless, completely dependent. Riska was in charge of our food, our surroundings, our communication with the rangers and the natural world. I left the cabin, closed the door behind me and threw the key in over the transom. The day before I had got badly sunburned — a result of

taking malaria medication and forgetting my sunscreen —
and now even daylight made me feel dizzy and sick. The hell
with it, I thought, and the hell with the danger. I was
indulging in a forbidden pleasure: NEVER GO OUT ALONE
AND ALWAYS NOTIFY THE RANGER. On the equator, night
comes suddenly. If something happened, if I disappeared,
got lost or eaten, no one would know where to look for my
remains. I was breaking the rules, but for a little while I'd take
charge of my life.

Out on the porch, I searched the camp area for any sight
of troublesome orang utans, but they were miraculously
absent. I moved away from the cabin and towards the trees.
You might not like the real me . . .

What was Riska hiding?

That night she presented me with a tape that she had
recorded alone in her room. "Don't listen until you get back
to Canada," she instructed, stalking into the dark kitchen
with a kerosene lantern to prepare our dinner of rice and
canned food while I began to think about Pandora's fatal
box. I put the tape away in my backpack and we didn't
mention it again. But something had changed. The dam had
broken and Riska began to talk more openly. When I left
Borneo the second time, I had about ten hours of her stories
on tape, and she had gradually modified the tone and even
the facts as we became more and more intimate. "I have a little girl," she told me when I returned from my solitary walk
on that hot, unhappy afternoon. "Nobody knows about her.
It is a secret part of my life."

She is a tribal person living in an alien culture, a culture that is not only modern but Muslim, a culture that shuns her people as barbaric. She has lost much in the process of coming downriver to live in a town, but in spite of that, she values knowledge above all else. Perhaps that's the crux of her dilemma, I thought. Her life doesn't fit in town or forest. She does not belong anywhere.

We had planned to spend the last five days of that second trip in Kudangan, but ended up in a Dayak village only about halfway there. To have gone all the way up to her birth village would have entailed a boat trip of several days or a drive of at least ten hours on an unpaved road, often made impassable by rain. Having seen both places now, I am glad to have visited Bakonsu first because it has no connection to the rest of the world except by boat and there are people there who have never seen people like me. In terms of our friendship, the time in that village was a turning point, since I was entirely out of my linguistic and cultural element and was more dependent on Riska than ever. This is a humbling situation to be in, but during our long conversations and enforced intimacy, we had begun to trust each other, to share many jokes and escapades and to move towards a partly common point of view that made us an "us" and everyone else a "them."

We arrived in Bakonsu with nothing but small backpacks and the food that we would consume while we were there, as well as a large tin of biscuits to share and some presents of notebooks and pencils for the children. We stayed in a longhouse with another woman and her three children. The *tuan*, husband, had been away for eight months cutting trees in the forest, but his wife took us in and I spent most of my time sitting on the floor of the longhouse (or, more properly "greathouse") which, being almost a hundred years old, was softening and rotting away over our heads and under our feet. There were gaping holes in the roof; on the wobbly floor there were plastic pails and one enormous antique jar to catch the rain that fell for a good part of every night and day. This water was used for cooking and making coffee, for washing dishes and brushing teeth. Otherwise we went to the river, which was down a steep slope close to the house. It was the slope we had climbed when we first disembarked and it was festooned, every few yards, with small platforms and thin flights of wooden steps. Twice each day one goes to the river to bathe, to wash the family clothes, to visit with neighbours, to use the tiny hut on the dock for a shit. The river moves fast. One's clothes, excrement or children are easily washed away.

The house is not properly a longhouse because it is inhabited not by an entire community, but by only one family. This is the way of the Ngaju and Tumon Dayak, as the government calls her mother's and her father's tribes, respectively. The bowed roof and slanted ironwood walls are more or less the same as in a traditional longhouse — of the sort build by the Dayak Iban, where many families live under one roof — but there is no long veranda along the side. Instead there is a simple one at the front which is reached by a notched log. Then there is a second notched log up to the door of the house. Generally the entire place is one room, with a kitchen area at the side or back and with slats in the wall to let the light in. As if they might float or fly or simply deconstruct, these houses are made without nails and all the parts move when touched — rounded floor boards, slatted walls, even rafters. They seem to live, to breath, to respond to the weight of hand or hip or foot.

While sitting on the bamboo floor, I loved to listen to Riska and Yefni's mother (called, in the Dayak way, according to her relationship to her oldest child). Although I could not understand the words they used, I could easily sense the mood of their talk, which involved lots of laughter and a great many stories. (Riska was known in that village through her grandfather, who had built the school with local help as he did in several other villages as well. When we went to the tuan's ladang one afternoon to help harvest rice, she was greeted by several old people as if her ties to Bakonsu were obvious.) One morning, when Yefni, the ten-year-old daughter, got up early and went out to play with a friend, she had an experience that she shared with her mother, who then shared it with anyone else who came by. The girls had gone to collect rubber, which is rolled into balls and used in competitions and games, in an area that is surrounded by several old graves. But that morning, Yefni saw what she later described to her mother as a "white leg only" climbing over a grave.

Each adult who visited the longhouse that day listened to Yefni or her mother recount the story and each asked Yefni about certain details. She was never suspected of concocting the tale or of believing in something unreal. She was respected as a person who had had an important experience, one that should be shared with others. I noticed that she had remarkable poise and self-assurance. I also noticed that she bore much of the responsibility for the daily chores of the household, that she washed herself and her clothes, deloused her own hair with the aid of a candle and mirror, cared for her brother and baby sister, took charge of certain meals. And now I began to see why. She was part of her community. It was as simple as that.

All in all the five-day visit to the village provided such a rosy glimpse of the culture Riska had been describing to me that I began to believe all Dayak communities were as Edenic as this one. I had been welcomed in a formal ceremony, complete with chicken, rice, gamelans and blood. I had observed an engagement ceremony, taken part in the hornbill dance, witnessed a house blessing that involved all-night prayers and spirit-defying shouts. I had been allowed to hold in my hands the human head that sat on a dish in the sandung across from our porch, and I had been taken through various graves by people who treated the bones of the dead as gently and fearlessly as if they were simply relatives taking long naps. I thought, Dayaks have been studied by ethnographers and anthropologists. They've been visited by tourists. But have they ever been described from the inside?

When it was all over, back in Toronto, I asked a friend to transcribe Riska's tapes. Of course there were decisions to be made. Should I retain any of my own questions? How much should I "correct" Riska's English, which was often intensely descriptive in its small inaccuracies? How much rearranging was appropriate? One of the options I considered was to have her tell her story in Bahasa Indonesia, the official language, which could be easily translated by somebody else. But the story she wanted to tell was always for "us" and Riska speaks "our" language, whereas I can't even begin to speak hers.

While I was struggling with these issues, I received a fat envelope from Pangkalan Bun, and suddenly the way to proceed was obvious. The material Riska enclosed had been written by a storyteller whose language and style on the page made our taped conversations pale by comparison. "My uncle was studying magic which he said was just to perfect himself," she wrote. "He was however a well-educated man. He was attending college and followed the study program from his office in many places. He was working as a *comat*, a leader of the district, in Balai Riam village. But on the other side, he absolutely believed there was power we could use by giving mantras and fulfilling the requirements. This uncle, he was younger than my father, and his wife was from a different Dayak tribe. They have their own language that is almost totally different from ours, and my uncle hated to be around his wife's family because when they talked he felt like a fool, not knowing what they were saying. . . ."

I began to look forward to those fat envelopes, which arrived every six weeks or so. I remember a particular line that convinced me she should write the stories herself. It was, "Her misery was solid," and it was eloquent and exactly to the point. I asked Riska to write all the stories we had taped and

I started the editing process again. There was no beginning, no middle, certainly no end. I was reading about the day before yesterday right along with distant memories and traditional ceremonies. When I decided to go back to Indonesia to see her again, Riska wrote, "I am happy to know that you will come between May and July. Also would be a good idea for you to visit my village where I was born."

This time she was writing from Bali, where she had, through an effort of will and ingenuity, gone to study German and Japanese. Her letters had become more self-conscious, in the sense that they were now written from a certain time and place and mood: "Dear Linda, thank you very much for the fax. I am writing this letter on the riverbank. A beautiful small river just a couple km from Ubud. It is just so peaceful here. The forest is just so green. Today is a big ceremony for Hindus. Men, women were dressing up nicely and colourful and the women were carrying basket offerings on their heads. Really early in the morning they were starting to prepare everything for the praying and going to the temple. I got a bit lonely today because most people were busy with their own business, so I took my push-bike and rode to Monkey Forest, then continued to Tundun village where I am writing now. Oh Linda, I remember my mom liked to make cake for us. . . ."

It seemed that she was warming up, in each letter, to her real subject. She would write pages and pages and pack them into an envelope. She had little money; even paying for the postage was difficult, but Bali had given her a sense of perspective that she had not had before. It released her from the constraints of her Kalimantan identity while making her more aware of it.

We were both looking forward to going back. I would be flying into Jakarta. She would fly in from Denpasar on Bali to meet my plane. Even this was an enormous change. It was hard to imagine her climbing onto an airplane so blithely. In fact, the sight of her in the vastness and confusion of the enormous airport in Jakarta was astonishing. I had always thought of her in the context of river and trees. Even Pangkalan Bun, where she'd grown up, seemed too urban for her exuberant personality. Now, in Jakarta for the next two days, it was not clear who was showing who around, as we were both strangers in this land. I was mired in the usual forbodings of missed messages and cultural misunderstandings, while Riska was dealing with the luxuries of high-speed living and a highrise hotel. All of it was thrilling to us in our separate ways.

Then together we boarded the little plane bound for Pangkalan Bun, where Riska would be reunited with her family and where we would rent a car and driver to take us, at last, to Kudangan.

Although Riska's mother protested that the trip was unsafe for a child, things went exactly as I had hoped and Riska's father and daughter came with us, which meant that four of us, instead of two, could be absolutely miserable for nine or ten hours. I knew Riska would hear things from her father that she might not hear otherwise, and I thought returning to the village with a daughter exactly the age she had been when she left would spark memories and emotions that might otherwise lie dormant.

The timber road on which we travelled was unpaved and deeply gouged by the weight of murdered trees — a weight that seemed to cling to everything we passed, along with dust, grime and physical ugliness. Everyone, with the exception, I suppose, of the driver, was carsick. Seven-year-old Karina threw up quietly and persistently for the entire trip, though the application of a certain sticky tape over her navel ("we believe it is the air going in that bothers the stomach there") seemed to bring some relief. Riska threw up as well, just as uncomplainingly, with Karina draped across her lap, while her father and I sat in the back, rolling the windows up whenever one of the timber trucks bore down on us spewing a grit so thick that we would be blinded and choked, and I would wonder why I had wanted to do this, what could possibly be at the end of this road that would make the misery worthwhile.

What was at the end of the road was Kudangan, and I am immensely glad to have seen it, to have seen the school where Riska's mother taught, to have bathed in the river where Riska almost drowned, and to have walked with her father as he showed me the church his own father built. Next to the church was an identical building, another church made to the same proportions and sporting the bell that had tolled in the first short steeple. It is the custom to replace a building rather than fix it, and the original is often left standing. I was glad to meet the young uncle, too, who has inherited all the family land and who has taken the wood off the frame of the grandfather's house to build a more modern equivalent. "That is the place where I used to sit looking out of the window," Riska said, pointing up at a vanished wall.

"Does it make you sad?"

"Only that the old house was so much better than this."

Riska had drawn me a rough picture of her family tree with so many uncle and aunty branches that I thought I would never keep them straight. Along with "village uncle: this one got the house and land," there was: "uncle who got killed," and "rich uncle who poked chickens," and "youngest uncle who won and lost 75 million." There was "youngest aunty, very spoiled, who said, 'you must never let your husband wash your underwear; it makes him a kind of idiot,'" and "mean aunty who said 'you only come here to eat'" and another aunty who "used to be very rich in Banjarmasin but let the business fail when her husband died and now sells old clothes up the river." Riska's father had eleven siblings. Her mother had ten.

I was glad to have seen the village, the river, the distant mountain of Sabayan, "where our ancestors go when they die," but something got under my skin on that timber road that no amount of bathing in the river could wash away. The river and forest were certainly beautiful. The sacred mountain appeared and disappeared. I tried to take photographs, but the horizon is always empty in those pictures and the village, flattened and reduced, looks oddly banal. Maybe that is the point. When we first arrived at the uncle's house, where no one was expecting us (since there is no way to send word), and where brothers and cousins had not seen each other for months or years, there was no fuss made at all. We simply climbed wearily out of our car (leaving the driver to his own devices) and staggered into the house where I was offered one of two rattan chairs and where, eventually, small cups of hot tea were served. We had brought food for ourselves and the requisite biscuits as gifts. At night everyone, including other unexpected guests, rolled out mattresses or mats and lay on the floor. There was one electric light which sometimes came on when the village generator worked, but for the most part, after seven or eight o'clock, it was as black as the proverbial pitch. Time to sleep. Life would begin again at dawn.

During the night every part of the floor was occupied and in the morning, as I made my way through the kitchen to the tiny adjacent toilet, I would step over the sleeping forms of whatever young men had stayed the night. Riska's brother, Leo, was with us for part of that week, as well as his friend, a man who has apparently lived in their small house in Pangkalan Bun off and on for years, though nowhere, as I remember, does he appear in Riska's narrative. This friend was thought to be wooing Riska's very pretty cousin except that they never spoke and showed not an ounce of interest in each other. "Are you sure?" I kept asking Riska.

"Oh yes. Oh yes!"

A few days before we left, he had to go back to town on his motorbike (a ride I don't want to imagine!) and the leave-taking made me suspect that Riska was right. Her cousin was bathing in the river, washing clothes impassively, when the motorbike and rider appeared just above us, on the bank, for a matter of perhaps ten minutes. She looked up. He looked down. He surveyed the river and perhaps thought of the long hours of bumpy road ahead. She bent and went back to her washing, and he watched her washing and then lifted a hand. That was it.

The river is the place to meet communally, but even here there is a sense of privacy, as if anyone, by invisible sign, can be alone. I was careful not to take my camera with me, feeling that in such a place it would be more invasive than it usually is, but on the last afternoon I couldn't resist. "Do you think it's all right?" I asked Riska, aiming it at two women who were crossing the river so far below us that I had to peer through the telephoto lens to make them out at all.

"They're too far away to see you," Riska said. But for once she was wrong. Both ladies lifted their sarongs, turned sideways, and bared their bottoms. One of them shouted something lustily.

"What'd she say?"

Riska laughed. "She said, 'Here's some real Kalimantan ass!'"

All this time I was noticing signs of whispery tension in the village although they weren't what was bothering me. Back on the timber road a rickety handmade barricade had been thrust out in front of us. It was not an official road-block, but we were all required to get out of the car and move around in a supplicatory pantomime. Later, as I learned more about the war between the Dayaks and Muslims — more particularly the Muslim transmigrants from the island of Madura — I realized that roadblocks were an obvious way to sort people out. "Are you from Madura? Prove that you're not!"

Strangely, the closer we got to Kudangan, the more signs of tension there were. "What's going on?" I kept asking Riska, as soldiers at an outpost just inside the village demanded to see identification, demanded bribes, demanded to follow me wherever I went — for my protection, they assured me.

"Against what?"

"Against us, the unruly and dangerous Dayaks," Riska said, asking me to please pay the bribe so the soldiers and local police would not bother her family. "I don't like it either," she admitted when I shook my head stubbornly. "But we could make things very hard for them here."

It was not until we were on our way to the ceremony that she said, "A lot of people were killed on a bus apparently. Left without heads. Not far from here. And it could spread. My father says not to talk. But it could happen here."

I had heard about the practice of passing what is known as the "Red Bowl" or "Cup" from one community to another. In this way the Dayak are called to war. What I didn't know was that even then the bowl was being passed. It is red with blood and decorated with chicken feathers. The ceremony we visited in the longhouse seems ominous, in retrospect, involved as it was with a bowlful of artefacts, the uncooked rice, into which a chicken was briefly bled, a lot of smoke and incense, and a good deal of praying by the chief of law.

Once the spiritual side of things was taken care of, I was invited into the circle of men. On such occasions I see myself without aid of mirror as gawky, off balance, ill-suited to my surroundings. But instead of a sensible invisibility, what is often pressed upon a traveller at such times is exactly the opposite. I was given a good deal of rice wine and taken out to the burial place of the village founder, on the way passing a newborn calf and a giant tortoise with a rope through a hole that had been drilled into its shell.

It was in this part of the village, which has over a thousand people, that I visited the most beautiful of Dayak graves — a tall and regal pyramid of five painted *tabaks* and much carving. Obviously someone important, I thought. "Here is the grave of another chief," I heard Riska say, but she was pointing to a smaller one, only three tabaks, with no fine carving.

"Then who is this?"

"His granddaughter. Oh, she was very cherished by him," Riska explained. "And she died when she was a child. My father knew her. They were the same age. She was born in 1943."

Behind us, Riska's father and daughter stood hand in hand. "Do you remember the little girl?" I asked him.

Riska translated. He nodded, holding Karina's hand a little tighter. In this village, in this way and in other ways, I learned of the great pleasure Dayak families take in their children. It is a pleasure that seemed too permissive to me at times, but it is abiding and unfettered and was made manifest on an afternoon when we had gone as a household (minus aunty) to a river far away for a picnic, the second event of the three that changed my view of Dayak life. Our trip involved the car and driver again, as well as any neighbours who could squeeze in. I did not notice any food or drinks being packed, but we all climbed in and drove off and eventually came, after an uphill climb, to a wooden bridge under which were some formidable rapids and a river paradise.

Within moments of alighting, wood was assembled for a fire. A pot emerged from someone's pack along with enough kernels of rice to provide us all with basic nourishment. When the fire was properly ablaze, water was brought up from the river and put to boil. Meanwhile, a boy who had come along from next door donned a homemade glass mask and went headfirst into the rapids with a very lethel-looking homemade speargun. In half an hour he had provided a bucketful of smallish fish that were cleaned by Riska's cousin, then packed with coarse salt and leaves into bamboo cylinders that Leo and his friend had cut from a nearby tree. Riska's father was fishing with a line. Her uncle was fishing with a net. After the chill of the water, there was hot tea to drink. The meal — steamed, grilled — was the most delicious picnic of my life.

From the shadows of the trees emerged men in loincloths. They had been cutting something in the forest. They waited politely for us to be done with our riverside meal, then accepted our offer of a ride down to the village. It was at this point that I received the lesson in community that I will never forget, for now, once everyone had got into the car and we were packed like river fish in a bamboo container, Karina objected to her position in the back seat. It seemed entirely unfair to her that her cousin, a child younger and less entitled, should be sitting on her grandfather's lap in the front while she was squeezed between three adult women and five men in the caboose. So saying, so explaining, she resorted to the kind of screaming, crying tantrum that would have earned unthinkable punishment in my natal house, so unthinkable that no such tantrum ever occurred in my own childhood or in my daughters' as far as I can recall. So unthinkable that I was immediately rigid with disapproval while Karina went on thrashing and even managed to throw up her lunch.

"Don't let her get away with this," I whispered to Riska when Karina yanked at the door handle in a futile effort to pull it off. I was a little embarrassed in front of the forest men who were crammed in behind us, afraid lest they feel they should get out and walk. Riska patted her daughter and wiped up the vomit. For a few moments, in fact, everyone within reach patted Karina, until her grandfather got out of the car and climbed into the over-crowded rear end where sat the uncle, the neighbours and the two forest men.

"We care about our children's happiness," Riska said firmly. It was a statement of conviction in a set of values that she recognizes as such. The values are a part of her that is not in conflict with itself and her calm assurance caused me to ponder my own outrage. Who was I *really* mad at? And why?

Of course it had nothing to do with Karina. It was adult passivity that I was raging at — adult passivity that concerned other activities altogether. That this was so became clear at last when we left Kudangan for good the next day, stopping at the army post near the entrance to the village to have our papers checked. I had to send my passport in with Riska and her father, and she asked me to put the equivalent of a few dollars in the back of it. This was the third momentous event. The money would be slipped under a book or some papers on the desk. Meanwhile I waited in the car, helpless again and increasingly furious. Karina's uncle had given her a puppy and I busied myself with it. Minutes ticked by. The car heated up. At last I opened the door and stepped out on the only stretch of poured concrete in the village — a stretch that led up to the army post. There were five or six soldiers standing on it and as I approached, two of them raised their rifles and aimed them at the village.

It was an act of such preposterous arrogance that it focussed my rage. The unpleasant feeling under my skin had been one of collusion in the dismantling of Dayak integrity. There is the timber road, with its nasty fumes and all the carcasses of great and ancient trees which it seems to consume. There are the soldiers who must come with the road and who have put up the long, blinking post at the door of the village, so that instead of being met by a chief and welcomed with ceremony, one is expected to hand over papers and a sufficient bribe in order to be "protected" from the forest-dwelling Dayaks who have, after all, been known to take heads, and who had now better hand over whatever is required including money and chickens and daughters so that the soldiers don't make their lives miserable.

The soldiers are outsiders. So are the timber men and so am I. No wonder a little ceremony was offered for the blessing of Kudangan as the nation known as Indonesia embarked on an election that would affect the lives of everyone born and raised under those trees, though thanks to the roads and the timber companies, the soldiers and politicians, half of the trees are gone now and Borneo is burning with fires that will not be quenched.

On the way back to Pangkalan Bun we stopped for a breath of fresh air, a stretch and a roadside pee in the middle of a mass of logs all cut and numbered and waiting to be taken away. It is the most desolate place I have ever been, for each log was the width of the car we'd climbed out of and five times as long. Each was part of an astonishing diversity that can never be re-created, that once lost is lost forever, and the sight of that loss all around us and of small, seven-year-old Karina with her long, fragile legs trying to scramble over those logs is something I'd like to forget. I watched Riska as she watched her daughter, and later, when I read her reactions to that sight, I knew we had seen it in the same way. I was impressed, in a way I had not been before, by the care she gave to everything she wrote. Although the story is, at times, deceptively simple, where Riska is reserved, she intends to be reserved. Where she is unveiled, she has considered the risk and written with acuity.

"Over there is the house my mother is buying with a government loan," she said quietly, as we came to the paved road that leads to Pangkalan Bun and passes first a tiny, very regimented community being built in the middle of nowhere on a treeless expanse outside of town. "I don't know why. What will they do out here?"

I thought, they will avoid the flooding of the Arut River and a few unfriendly neighbours. They will pretend for a while that they are in the countryside again. But it will only be a patch of ground where once there was a forest.

We didn't stop. We hurried on. We were going to spend three days on the Sekonyer River, among trees in the national park. And we were going to keep working on our books. Hers and mine. There was no longer any question of shyness or secrets or force or control. We would lie on our mats in the belly of the boat and talk for hours. Draw maps. Exchange information, knowledge, opinions, points of view. Then I was going to go back to Toronto; Riska would go back to Bali. We would stay in touch one way or another. We would each affect the other in countless ways.

A pleasant equality had come over us during Karina's post-picnic tantrum. It had come over us when Riska said, "We care about our children's happiness," and I recognized my self-righteousness and saw that it was ill-founded. I had not realized, until that moment, that I had been disapproving of more and more things ever since we'd arrived. With Karina and her cousin in the front seat together and the car beginning its slow descent to Kudangan, I remembered the visible anger with which I had thrown a discarded battery out of the river and onto the shore while we had been bathing. I remembered the way I had ostentatiously cuddled the puppies that Riska's uncle had chased out of his house and the way I had clucked over the treatment of the tortoise tied to a tree. Once recognized, my sense of outrage over things in the village suprised me. Apparently this was not the idyllic nest I had expected. I had wanted the villagers to live up to my expectations. I had wanted the forest to be uncut. I had wanted no sound of chainsaws to meet my ears. And if there were to be soldiers in camouflage uniforms, I suppose I had wanted the noble Dayaks to cut their throats.

❊

The last piece of mail I received from Riska was her own version of our trip to Kudangan, and I have closed her book with it because it answered so many of the questions I had: What's all the whispering about? How dangerous is our situation? Some of those questions had been answered by Richard Lloyd Parry, a reporter with the *Independent* in London, who had seen headless human remains and evidence of "an ethnic war of scarcely imaginable savagery, fought according to ancient principles of black magic." But others, more particular to our visit, were unravelled by Riska as she described our journey.

Dayak warriors are known for their ability to withstand bullets, to go into a trance that makes them impermeable to the realities of combat and the imprecations of conscience, but this was no traditional headhunting raid. Men, women and children were massacred and beheaded in Kalimantan that winter and spring. Something had gone terribly wrong, and after reading the accounts that were finally published months after I left, it seemed more miraculous than ever to be given, first hand, the story of someone who is half inside that tradition, a woman with her feet planted firmly in two worlds, and who describes, so vividly, just what has been lost in the swift transition from tribal life to the modern world.

Riska's written words have been changed as little as possible. As editor, I worked to make tenses consistent and to regularize usage where it seemed necessary. For the most part I found her sentences too interesting as they stood to bear much tampering. In arranging the many anecdotes, I opted for chronology — a simple mirroring of experience, since her narration had come to me piecemeal in letters. Hoping initially to tell the "true story" of her people, Riska does not, I think, see her life as emblematic. "Maybe I should not use my name," she wrote, after editing the final draft. Then, in a postscript she added, "But I don't know. If I write this, and it does not have my name, how can I be proud? It's my book, isn't it?"

Linda Spalding
Toronto, 1999

Riska

The Secret Parts of Life

There is a legend about a young Dayak hunter named Sangi who lived on the Mahoroi. He was good with his blowpipe and every time he went hunting he killed an animal and brought it home. But one day he went to the forest and could not find any animal to kill. On his way home, at the end of the day, he noticed that the water by the riverbank was cloudy. An animal had been drinking there. A wild boar.

The hunter decided to follow the tracks of the animal and soon he saw the wild boar, but he was terrified at the sight. The poor wild boar was already dead . . . and in the mouth of a giant snake. Sangi hid behind a bush and watched as the snake tried to swallow the wild boar. But, choking and gasping, the snake always failed.

Suddenly the snake changed his appearance and became a handsome young man. He strode to Sangi's bush and with a hypnotizing voice said, "You dare to watch me!" Then, cursing Sangi, he said, "and now I will turn you into a snake."

But the giant snake told Sangi that although he would be a snake at night, he would stay young forever; he would never die. But he must never tell anyone his secret.

He tried to hide his secret from his family, but secrets are hard to hide! The family wanted to know why he stayed so young. They rained questions on him constantly until one day he broke the taboo. Little by little, as he told them his story, his body changed. Toe to head, scales appeared. Fangs. When he realized this, he blamed his family. He cursed them, saying they would die fighting each other. He took the family's antique jars full of their gold and jewels, and threw them into the river. Then he leapt in the river himself.

According to some people who make a journey past that river, there is a snake with a head as big as an oil drum who comes to the bank when a full moon comes out. People don't dare to do any mining there, even though the river is rich with gold. And, of course, Sangi's family all died. The story shows us how unkind it is to want to know someone's secret. To want to destroy the secret parts of life.

1

At the Head of the
Delang River

A LONG TIME AGO the chief of our tribe, Jajar Melahui, wanted to discover the place where we should
live. He made a *todung* ceremony, and released three coloured
partridges in three directions, thinking he would establish
the boundaries of our village where they landed. But the
birds flew into an area which is sacred and forbidden. Very
forbidden. You could not enter; you could not build a house
in that area. So the partridges confused the tribe.

Jajar Melahui was thinking and thinking, over and over,
and finally when he slept, he dreamed that he must follow the
instructions of the birds and build the village in the area they
had flown into even though it is forbidden. In his dream, he
saw a big village, a centre of government — and now, in that

place, there are a thousand people. Kudangan, the name of this place where I was born, means "the place of the partridge," the sacred bird of paradise. I was born at the head of the Delang River, among the people of the Dayak Tumon tribe. My grandparents, my parents and the people of the village were wholly dependant on the rich soil for making their *ladangs*. They watched the birds for signs of how to behave. Do we hunt today? Or travel? There I spent eight years of my childhood out of touch with modern life.

I was born in this village up the Delang River on September 21, 1969. I had my childhood in the village and began my education there in the school my grandfather built, where my mother was a teacher. My father hunted for wild boar and deer. He also tapped rubber trees and made palm sugar. The longhouses in the village are similar to the longhouses in Sumatra because once the village was settled and became the district centre, a Sumatran warrior named Patih Sebatang, arrived. He had fought with the Dutch on the island of Sumatra and lost a battle. He ran away, crossed the sea to Borneo and, chased by his enemies, came up the river. He managed to hide in our village. The warrior married a beautiful Dayak girl and they had a son. That's why we have a kind of mixture between the culture from Sumatra and the Dayak Delang. And we have the evidence of this — a *keris* spear that belonged to the warrior and also a flag from his kingdom of Pagar Ruyung. They're still on exhibit. They are our village heirlooms.

Most of the Dayak live in the hinterland along the Lamandau River, the Delang River, the Batangkawa and Belantikan.

Kudangan is near the border of West Kalimantan in a mountainous area. From there you can see Mount Sabayan in the distance, our deep heaven, along with two of her younger sisters. My tribe is very small. We were dependant on the forest for our medicine and for the material to build our longhouses. We were children using the forest as our playground. I never dreamed, as a child, that the forest could change, could disappear. All our stories and customs come from the forest. All the *adat* — our laws.

Dayak people call themselves by the names of their rivers. My father is Dayak Tumon — that's a government designation. He was born in the same village as me so the people say he is Dayak Delang. He spent time in my mother's town to finish high school, which was very difficult at that time, and there he met the beautiful girl with very long hair and light skin who was about to finish her training to be a kindergarten teacher. They fell in love and decided to marry when my mother finished her studies.

When he was a student my papah had to leave his parents in Kudangan and live with relatives in town who were not rich. Every morning he had to wake up early and do all the kitchen duty, cooking for the family members, washing and cleaning the house before going to school. For breakfast, he would get the rice that was left in the cooking pan. Mostly if we cook rice, there is some left half-burned in the bottom of the pan. So that's what he got for his hungry stomach. He never had enough food and had to work hard just to get a small space to sleep. But his spirit was so high that he finished his studies.

My mamah (her name is Anne) is Dayak Ngaju. She tried to convince her parents that Papah was a good man and came from a very good family and that they originally came from the same tribe, but her parents said my father, whose name is Belle, came from the Delang River. It was a shame to marry someone from his village.

My mamah's feelings were hurt. The village where she lived was called Pahandut. Later, after our Independence Day, the government changed the name to Palangkaraya. They built tall monuments in the middle of the town, which began to grow very fast and established itself as the administrative capital of Central Kalimantan. My mamah used to tell her children about that village with longing and sadness. I think it would embarrass her to have her children know her story. In our family the relationship between a man and a woman is not discussed. We don't talk about it. She just says she went to high school and got training to be a teacher and then she met my father and got married. She and her new husband left her village after their marriage. She was only seventeen and my papah was only nineteen. I heard once from my sister, who now lives in Palangkaraya and married a man from a different tribe, that before he married, Papah was engaged to a beautiful girl he did not love. His parents chose her for him, but he loved my mother.

My father told his parents that he wanted to be in the army but his parents did not allow this. They said to be in the army means to be ready to die at any moment because our government sends men to war, to the battlefield. But he could do anything else, and his father offered to find him a government job. My father said he would never get a job from the government. He didn't want it because my grandfather would not let him be in the army. He would work as a farmer and hunter. In the village there was no place for buying meat, so my father would hunt and then sometimes sell meat to people who needed it. And also he would tap my grandfather's rubber trees.

My grandfather was building schools and other places and he was given land in our village and across the river until he had a very large *ladang*. It was about 800 hectares. He planted the land with rubber and coffee and fruit trees working by himself or hiring people to work for him. My grandpa was the first person to grow wet rice in that village, and our rice barn was always full. He was also a teacher. Some of his students told us that he was very strict, a disciplinarian. He would give his students a fishing line to fish so they would try to find something for themselves and not get it easily without effort. That's why, when I was small and always eating bananas he would ask, "Do you like it? Is it good?" If I said, "Yes," then he said back, "If it's good, then plant it." For a long time, when there was no school building yet, he was a travelling teacher. He taught from one village to another without complaining. Everything he did by walking, passing through the jungle on a small path called *jalan tikus*, which means rat road, because it's so small. Sometimes it would take a day to walk to the nearest village crossing small rivers on the slippery wooden bridges made of big round logs which had fallen across the water. There were thousands of leeches along the way. But he never gave up. Finally he got a contract from the government to build a school. It was U-shaped with six classrooms.

He also built the church, a small clinic and a house for the head of the district.

Most of our houses are made of ironwood. Our men collect the wood from the deep part of the jungle, cutting it with an axe and making it into nice pieces which take many weeks to finish and then carrying them to the river where they make a raft of the pieces and bring them to the village. Many people now use iron nails for building a house but many also still use rattan to put it together. We use ironwood to build high stilts and bark for the walls and areca wood for the floor. A longhouse doesn't have any windows. It's plain, with no rooms, you just go directly to the kitchen. Sometimes it's quite dark and damp so many people have problems with disease. Longhouses have no rooms because people need the long space for feasts even though it means no privacy. Some Dayaks now use mosquito nets — that's their only privacy.

My grandpa — Bue is what we called him, and Tambi for grandma — built a house on stilts but it was a bit different from the others around it. It had a window and a small room in the back. That is where we lived, in the same house with my grandparents.

In our kitchens we use firewood. Above the stove we have a shelf where we can keep many things like wood, or a place for smoking fish and meat. Sometimes there is a big jar full of salt. Salt is a very holy thing, very expensive. Salt is just like gold. We keep it over years, so it tends to be very hard, like stone. Often we have goitre, because we mostly use salt without iodine.

In the morning when I woke up I loved to see my mother cooking on the fire stove. Our kitchen was quite big. I loved to sit in the window, squatting, looking outside. Our house was built on high stilts and next to it were some fruit trees. When the season was right, I could see fruit on them. I owned a small star fruit tree just next to the house, so if other people wanted to have some fruit they had to ask me first. My younger sister, Lilis, owned another star fruit tree but hers was very high so not so many people liked to ask for her fruits and also her tree was full of a stinging insect we call *sesu* in my mother's language or *kaho* in Delang.

My parents had left Mamah's village in 1962 after their marriage. They'd departed from Banjarmasin, a main town in south Kalimantan, because the harbour was there. The journey was long, crossing the sea. A boat the size of a tug, twenty-five metres long, took two days to arrive in Pangkalan Bun. They came up to Nanga Bulik, a Malay village, while waiting for Mamah's working contract as a teacher. Her first baby was born there a year later, and my mamah was taken care of by a nun and a pastor who ran a clinic. She used to tell us how well the German nun took care of her.

After that they came up to Kudangan, where Mamah became a teacher in 1964. My papah was tapping rubber, tapping palm to make sugar, growing coffee and cloves, fishing and hunting as well. I remember once he came back from hunting carrying a big rattan backpack we called *ladung*. It was full and heavy. Inside was a big wild boar. My papah had cut it in big slices so it was easy to carry. Later on some neighbours came and helped him clean the meat. They helped burn the hair in the flames. While working they cooked rice and grilled the liver. We had a small party in the kitchen. They were eating and talking until midnight and sharing stories and experiences. Some brought rice wine and they drank together.

Papah used to tell us how to hunt: first we had to have good dogs which were well trained and had good hunting sense. Then we had to find a place where wild boar or deer visit such as an old ladang or a drinking place. We had to go sometimes at night, carrying a spear. If there is any wild boar or deer in the distance, a good hunting dog can smell it and start barking and chasing. A good hunting dog will chase and try to block the way so the animal will get confused and panic. Then my father could come closer and stab the animal with his spear. He said a wild boar is the most dangerous animal in the jungle. They eat everything from small animals to human beings. He told us to avoid a wild boar if it is attacking by running zigzag and hiding behind a big tree. The boar will always run straight and can't turn around suddenly.

Hunters who were after smaller animals, such as mouse deer, birds and monkeys, used blowpipes, which is a traditional Dayak weapon along with the *mandau*, our traditional sword. Our blowpipe is made from ironwood. We choose a good wood then shape it round and long, sometimes up to two-and-a-half metres in length. Then we use an iron stick to make a hole and drill it little by little.

It can take months to finish one blowpipe. Sometimes the iron stick goes the wrong way and we must cut the pipe, although Dayak people prefer to have a long one. On the tip they put a spear and hold it with rattan rope. There is no painting on it. It's plain.

Some early mornings, after having a cup of sweet coffee, Papah would go to the ladang across the river to tap the palm flower before sunrise and bring us big jars of the juice. The juice we call *lahang*. My mamah would filter it to get out the flies' carcasses or the fibre that was mixed in, then she would give us some as a fresh drink. After that, my papah would put a big iron frying pan on the fire and pour the juice in it. Some hours later there would be a sticky, palm-fragrant liquid. When the juice got brown and creamy, Mamah would stand bamboo cyclinders about three centimetres high on a tray and pour the thick cream into them.

I loved to help her. I could choose one and shake the container so the round sugar dropped out of the hole. Mamah warned me not to shake it out until it was cool or I would damage the shape and burn my fingers. I liked the warm cream because it was sweet and my mouth couldn't stop licking it off my fingers. If we got a lot of palm sugar blocks, my mamah would store them in the jars or pack them in palm leaves in a special place over the firestove. That way, the sugar would stay safe from mushrooms. My grandfather loved to have creamy hot cereal made out of brown rice flour and Mamah cooked it in the big pan on the firestove and mixed in coconut milk and a lot of palm sugar. She made spoons for us out of young coconut leaves.

When we had durian season, my papah would go to the ladang or the forest to collect the durian that had fallen from the tree. The fruit is as big as a coconut and thorny. He would carry his big rattan pack home full and we sometimes ate it directly. It has a sharp and fragrant smell. Often our neighbours barter durian for salt or seasoning. We can make salty durian if we have salt. We use small thin pieces of bamboo and take the flesh from the seed. When the tin basin is full of fruit, my mamah mixed in some salt, saying we have to put the right amount in to give the right taste. If we put less salt, the durian will taste very sour and won't last long. But if we put too much salt, it will be bitter. We'd put it in jars and it would keep for many months, even years. If my papah got fish, my mamah would boil it and mix an amount of salty durian in along with lemon grass, ginger, crushed saffron, fresh crushed pepper, some chillies, a bit of fish paste and seasoning. It was very tasty and spicy.

One day I met some of my friends and we agreed to go to my grandfather's land across the river where we had some durian trees. So we went down to the river close to my house and I let my friends use my father's ironwood canoe to cross to the other side. The canoe was long and heavy and the stream was very fast. I was sitting up front and helping to paddle, struggling to keep the front of the canoe in the right place. The water was clear and cool and not deep so we could see the small dark stones at the bottom of the river and some small fishes called *kendompang* moving everywhere when our canoe passed them on the surface.

When we arrived on the other side of the river, we tied the canoe rope to a small tree and ran to the old ladang. I didn't use any sandals because I did not have any so my feet sometimes hurt from rattan thorns which were scattered on the trail but I didn't care. If I got thorns in my feet I put papaya sap on the thorns and let it dry before I used pincers to take them out. I was happy to suffer for durian!

Sometimes, my father took me out to his friend's ladang. He helped him plant seeds with other people, then he taught me how to catch pompi, a black, spider-like animal who lives in the holes of the ladang after it's burnt down. The pompi hole is ten centimetres deep. We used to tickle the hole with a piece of small bamboo to get them out. When we catch one we press him to the ground with a piece of wood then break the teeth because they are poisonous. Most Dayak people are fond of this food. They fry it or cook it in a bamboo cyclinder. It's a Dayak delicacy.

Mamang beruang are bigger than pompi. Their hole is twenty to thirty centimetres deep and their colour is pink to reddish. Their teeth are also poisonous.

Dayak people eat almost everything. We enjoy monkey meat, orang utan meat, snake, frog, palm larva, grasshoppers, snails. My eleven-year-old cousin sometimes hunts for snails at night. At a certain season they eat the plants in the garden so she goes out in the night with a bamboo torch and searches under the plants. She collects the snails in a basket and next morning she will be very busy making satay out of them. She breaks the house of the snail and takes the meat out and puts them all in a basin and mixes in salt. The snails can't stand the salt and die. My cousin then mixes a little lime from betel nut and kneads the meat with it in order to get rid of the mucous membrane. She keeps it like that a little while before she washes it off. Then she cuts the meat in pieces, sticks them on bamboo sticks and uses some spices such as crushed onion, saffron and pepper, and grills them on the firestove. Her mother gets sick of seeing her eat snail meat, but my cousin always says it's delicious.

When we were in Kudangan, fishing was still easy. Papah sometimes went out in the night in his dugout canoe bringing his fishing net and by midnight brought home strings of big fishes. Then for breakfast we ate rice with fish fried in homemade coconut oil. Papah got his own baked fish crushed with fresh chillies and fish paste. But the last time I went up, staying with my aunty, she was complaining that there were almost no fish left to catch in the river. My auntie's son Deka often had to go far upriver to catch fish with his homemade needle gun and homemade glass mask. It is true that the somah, a huge fish that once lived along the Delang River is almost gone. I still remember the time Papah went fishing and came back in the night with a huge somah fish. I woke up in the morning and found the fish hanging by a small rattan line in the middle of the kitchen. We loved the meat. It's very fatty and tasty and the fish can grow up to one metre long and as big around as a medium coconut trunk. It was fortunate to get this fish. If we went fishing, it was taboo to mention the word somah. It was holy and would bring bad luck if we were not careful to respect its name. Sometimes, when I was small, some naughty boys teased us and shouted from the riverbank saying, "Are you going to catch SOMAH fish?" We were furious.

If I went with Papah to our ladang, without care, with leeches sucking on my legs, I played and inspected the places that interested me. Next to our ladang was an old coffee field. The trees were tall and anty but there was a lot of fruit, so I filled my small basket with coffee. Mamah would dry the beans in the sun for a couple of days and pound them in the rice mortar to peel off the outer skin. After they were clean she fried them without oil until they turned black and burned. She mixed a handful of rice or corn in the frying pan. It smelled good. My mamah said the rice would reduce the bitterness and make the coffee more tasteful. But my papah did not like it if there was too much rice in it. Mamah would then pound it in the wooden rice mortar to make coffee powder. It was fun to see the pile of coffee powder in the tin tray but Mamah was annoyed every time I played there, piling it and shaping it like a pyramid so that some of it got scattered on the floor. Sometimes I sat on the end of the giant rice mortar which was shaped like a ship, shaking and bumping from the activity while my mamah pounded the coffee.

When Papah went down to the town selling coffee or cloves from our ladang, Mamah and all of us children had to stay behind. He went on his boat without any motor or on a bamboo raft and the journey would take many days. To come back he would paddle or with some companions he would take the faster way and walk along the riverside passing one village and then another with a heavy load on his back, his pack full of presents for his children and daily needs like sugar, salt, some spices, batteries, clothes and other things. I was always proud of my father because I thought he was so superior. I always loved to be with him. When I cried, sometimes I cried just to get his attention and he would pick me up and try to comfort me.

Our house was a bit isolated from other houses and Mamah sometimes got a bit scared to be alone with seven children. The closest house was on the other side of the road but it was always empty because the owners spent most of the time in their ladang. The other close longhouse was a hundred metres away, a place used to hold funeral ceremonys because it was big enough to hold the whole village. When someone died, the body would be immediately moved to that house for weeks or even months. At night we could hear women crying, a kind of crying we called *kumang rawa*. It was more like a loud song, with talking between the crying about the dead person. Every woman who came to console had to go to the coffin, sit down and start this crying. Nowadays, since the missionaries came and many local people changed their Kaharingan faith to be Christian, we don't often find these ceremonies because only some old people have kept their original faith. Once they die, all the ceremonies and parties will be finished and we'll only tell our children stories about the golden time when hundreds of people gathered and gave their complete respect to someone who died. They'll never witness these golden days of their own people, our own original faith. There will be no more days and days of parties with rice wine.

Anyway, during the times Papah was down the river, Mamah sent one of us children to pick up Indai Simin (Mother Simin), an old widow who lived next to the football field. She was short and a little fat and lived alone in her small longhouse. We asked her to come and stay with us for as long as Papah was gone. Indai Simin was a soft and kind woman blind in one eye. She and Mamah were good friends. One night when all of us stayed together after dinner, I asked Mamah why Indai Simin had a blind eye, and Mamah told me that she had an accident when she went to her ladang one day and had to pass some tall grass that covered a small patch of ground. "The sharp blades of grass poked her eye accidentally and she's been blind in that eye since then," Mamah said, as we sat by the floor under the dim light of the kerosene lamp. Indai Simin just nodded her head while quietly chewing her betel nut. Sometimes she moved the mat a little, bowed and then spat her blood-red saliva through the small chink in the floor. When we children went to bed, Mamah and Indai Simin usually talked till late before she finally laid out her kapok mattress on the floor in the middle of the room. Early in the morning, after a glass of coffee, she would go back to her own home then to her ladang outside of the village, and come back in the afternoon. She'd wait for one of us to pick her up again to spend the night until Papah came back from the town bringing sugar, salt and seasoning for Mamah and sweets for us and some tobacco bars for himself.

Papah used to roll his tobacco in corn leaves on his thigh. But then he stopped. He preferred chewing betel nut. We had many areca nut trees in the back yard and my sisters and I used to collect the bright red areca fruit for him from the ground. He would open it with his *kancip*, the traditional iron tool used to open the nut. It was actually my grandma's kancip. I sometimes tried to use it and when Tambi saw me, she would forbid it. She said it was taboo for children. "If you cut yourself with that, you have to pay the one who owned the kancip with a male chicken to clean the bad luck from the blood." I argued with her and asked why I had to pay her a chicken if I cut myself. I thought I was the one who needed to get a chicken because of the suffering I would bear, but my grandma did not explain the reasons further and just took the kancip away.

My mother says that my papah has friends who always accompany him, that they are invisible spirits. She says that he sometimes behaves strangely, as if he is having a conversation with someone he can't see, and that when Papah was still a kid, he learned from a guru about *silat*, which deals with invisible power. Little Papah learned how to control the inner power centralized in the body. The guru bathed him with flowers and mantras in the river. Papah did not know the meaning but since then he has power that protects him from all the bad spirits that try to enter his body.

My mamah would say that she married an "Orang Delang," a man from the Delang River, the place where the Dayak Tumon come from as well as her children, since her second baby and all the others were born in my papah's village. But she was happy if someone said that we are from the Ngaju tribe, the tribe of glory and high culture. At school we learned our national language Bahasa Indonesia but in our house, we must speak my mother's language. My parents would be very angry if we talked to them in another language except Ngaju. People teased my mamah if she spoke Dayak Tumon, as she could not really pronounce it well. Dayak villages have different languages. I speak two Dayak languages plus Indonesian . . . and English!

My mamah told me that Delang women are disloyal to their husbands and change partners very easily. There was a practice with government officials who came to the village that they would be given a girl as a present for one night. The girls would be made up nicely and the one who got chosen would be honoured to do her duty. My mamah told me that you could get a girl by approaching her parents and offering them a bar of tobacco. They would let you have their daughter for one night.

I have three brothers (Eby, Uber and Leo) and three sisters (Arita, Lilis and Yayang). I'm in the middle. We were all born in my grandparent's house at the head of Delang River except for my oldest brother, Eby, who was born in Nanga Bulik down the river, in the Catholic clinic run by the German missionaries. We grew up among the Tumon tribe, which my mamah said had lower culture than the tribe she came from, although she never mentioned that to other people. In a way my tribe is more old-fashioned. In my mother's tribe they don't have many ceremonies, but we have gods in the river and we have gods who stay in a big tree or in stones. And in the mountain. Our highest god we call *Sanghyang Duato*. We put our offerings in small rattan baskets and hang them on a pole near the river. Yes. At the center of our life was this one thing, the river. Always, it was part of us.

2

A Day to Give Offerings

WHEN I WAS SMALL, the time I loved best was when I could accompany my mother to the river. I used to help her wash clothes on flat stones with a piece of soap. She would carry a large tin basin full of dirty clothes. The tin basin was precious because it had to be purchased down the river. She used a bar of soap which had stinking and spicy aromatics. Then she bathed herself and rubbed a flat stone on her skin. She wore long clothes which fit tight around her body.

I never saw my mamah bathing nakedly like most women in the village did. They would take off all their clothes and cover their secret parts with their hands before jumping in the river. If the women were bathing, the men moved downriver and bathed naked too. But my mamah was a respected teacher in the village so there was no way for her to bathe nakedly, and my papah never did either. He always bathed in his worn shorts, but one thing special about my papah is that he very seldom took a bath. Mamah said he could go for a month without having a *mandi* and he would not smell. My mamah said that he could do that because of the invisible spirit which stayed in his body. The more seldom someone bathes, the higher his power is. My papah's guru long ago had filled his body with power and granted him a good spirit which covered and protected him.

The village women caught small fishes in baskets or *tangguk*, woven from bamboo or seloban bark. I remember that I really wanted to have a small tangguk, so I tried to make one for myself. I took bamboo and sliced it thin and tried to weave it. Even though it was shapeless, I brought it when Mamah was washing in the river and I caught tiny fishes under small stones with my own tiny basket. The second one I got as a present from my aunty — a small beautiful tangguk made from seloban bark she'd gathered from our old ladang. She saw my tangguk and promised to make small ones for my sister and me. Mine was very neat and very beautiful and I was so happy.

My sister sometimes sneaked off and joined her friends catching fishes upriver by the shallow rapids, but I was too young. Mamah told us it was very dangerous for girls. Once a woman from Nyalang village, who had just given birth a week before, wanted to eat fish so she went to the river with her woven basket. Her husband asked her not to go but she insisted. She got some fish and then the day came when she felt sick and restless and started to bleed. The bleeding got worse and there was no doctor. They had to bring her to Kudangan. Although we did not have a doctor either, we had some local people working with limited medicines brought from the town. But before anyone managed to get the woman to us, her bleeding got worse and she passed away. Later on, rumour said that when she caught fish in the river by the grass and rocks, a leech entered her womb and sucked her inside. She bled to death.

Still, I liked to search for tiny shrimps under the river stones. I'd catch them by hand and eat them alive, five or six at a time. They were sweet in my mouth. Our old people told us to do this if we wanted to swim like a shrimp, so after I swallowed the shrimp I would go to a place where the water was not too deep or fast and I drowned myself many times and drank lots of water. The water was so clear that I loved to drown my face in it and watch the small fishes. I did this until my eyes hurt and I was out of breath. My mamah asked me many times to stop it, but I loved to watch my fingers looking bigger and funny under the water. My nose was in pain and my eyes were stinging but I kept trying.

When I was five years old and trying to learn how to swim, I went with my friends to the rapids and I just slipped off the sand. A piece of bamboo had floated by and I stuck out my hand to grab it but I was small and it was out of reach. Then I slipped and the dark water sucked me in. I didn't know how to swim and a whirlpool sucked me and twisted me down. I couldn't breathe, I couldn't cry. I tried to grab something on the surface. A man who was taking a bath there saw my hand grabbing at the surface and he jumped in and saved me from the whirlpool. It happened so fast. I remember standing by the river, naked, shaking, out of breath, and the man telling me to go home.

In the afternoon I went back to the place where I was almost killed and I saw my father with some people by the river making a ceremony. My father had given a chicken to the person who saved me.

My mamah told me that when she was a girl, a medicine man had noticed a sign that one of the girls in the family would die in the river, killed by a crocodile. The sign was an invisible lizard on her face. The lizard's features started at the forehead and came down gradually toward the mouth. It takes some years before it reaches the mouth, but the marking was almost completed although nobody could see the mark except somebody who was granted extra senses. The girl was lucky. The family hurriedly made a ceremony for her. The medicine man brought the girl in the evening to the river and bathed her there with flowers and mantras. Then the girl jumped in the river and stood in the deep water and she told her family that when she stepped in the cold river, her feet touched a rough surface underwater. The water was deep and there was no way her feet could touch the bottom. The rough surface was something moving. She was sure that she was standing on the back of a huge crocodile. And the lizard marking was gone.

And Mamah told me that once her little niece was missing in the afternoon. Her parents were worried and looked for her, but had no success. They almost lost hope when somebody saw something floating under the house, which stood on high stilts. The house was built over the river and the water was high. The parents were hysterical to find out that it was their little girl's body. People took the body from the water where she had been for hours. The body was cold. The other family members held the mother who was trying to touch her girl but an old man, a distant relative, told her not to touch the body because the spirit would not come back if a close family member touched it. The old man carried the body upside down on his shoulder with the head down and the legs up and he ran with the body like that. He kept running making circles around the house. When evening fell, he stopped and the body moved. Water was dripping. My mamah said the little girl died at the time and is alive by a miracle now. She is alive today and has a family. Her spirit came back.

This story also reminds me of something I saw in my village when the river flooded. The water was rising furiously. We had a big rain upriver and all the water was sent down. My neighbours went in the morning to the ladang across the river. The mother brought her little girl with her. The water was quite high, but they kept crossing it in a small wooden canoe. There was a sudden roar and the strong-moving flood rushed down from the head of the river crushing the canoe. The little girl was thrown out and gone in a second in the angry stream. The terrified mother witnessed her little girl gone.

The villagers found the body down the river. For a couple of days I saw the mother walking to and fro by the riverside where her little girl had drowned, crying loudly and crushing the grass she passed with a long knife. Her misery was solid and her wailing kept haunting my mind. For some days the air was filled with mourning. We believe if somebody is taken by the river it means that we did not give enough offerings to the god who owns the river. He got angry and demanded a sacrifice. The medicine man should have led a ceremony and given an offering.

My mamah told me that the girl who died was the most beautiful girl in the family. She was only seven at the time.

In dry season we had a day to give offerings to the river. There was a big party, music all day and lots of people went down to *topin durai*, the rapids where the chief was muttering some mantras. Sometimes his voice would be very low and hardly heard, then suddenly it would be louder and faster, with *bahaso duato*, god language, which I hardly understood. As he spoke, he started sowing rice in the river. When he finished, he went to a small building made of bamboo where we kept the offerings. He was muttering again and some people handed him the offerings to put in — rice, eggs, rice wine, baked chicken, sticky rice. After praying one more time, they left and went back to the party.

What we do in the village depends on the season. When we make the ladang, we cut the trees and leave them awhile till they dry and then we burn them off and it produces ash to fertilize the soil. We wait until just before the rainy season and then we plant. When we're planting, it's in dry ground.

We make a small hole and put the seed in it, and let it grow. We are wholly dependent on the rain. It's a tradition that when somebody opens a new ladang, others will come and help, so everything will be finished within a couple of days. After that, the others will have their turn. For the honour of the ladang, when people work the whole day, it's a duty to feed them. And then at night, if they have a little money, they can make a party. At first, we grow corn among the rice, and sometimes watermelons. Then the party!

Sometimes we have a few areas planted with sticky rice. *Rondang* is a kind of snack we make from this when it's almost ripe. We fry it in a pan without oil then pound it in the rice mortar to take off the husk. We can eat it with palm sugar and grated coconut. *Sango* is a special cake made of brown rice. The rice flour is mixed with sugar then fried, just for special occasions. It's taboo to say the word "sango" if we don't have any, otherwise we will be cursed and become sick. *Lomang* is brown sticky rice cooked in a bamboo cylinder with coconut milk and a little salt. Wrapped in banana leaves, it produces a wonderful smell.

At harvest time, everybody in the village looks happy. Almost every night we have a party with the hornbill dance, new rice and chicken and pork. Sometimes those things only show up at a party. Many jars of newly made or old rice wine are favourites. And lomang. Very delicious.

When we have a full moon, lots of young people go out and sing together. *Berayah* is a kind of song that sounds very jolly, with four lines and different words depending on the situation. It sounds something like this:

Tulak lah, tulak ke hulu sungai
Babalah bubu hondak bajolu
Apa daya hati marangai
Kawalpun jouh hati marindu,
Kawalpun jouh hati marindu.

In the village, we celebrated Christmas in the small church on the hill. At night, my father held a bamboo torch to see the road. There were many people in the church and we got to sit in front because my parents were respected. We sat in wooden seats side by side. In front, on each side, stood two wild pine trees, their peaks touching the roof. We decorated them with candles on every branch. The tick, tick sound from the burning needles was wonderful. People were singing, led by the priest. And praying. After the praying we went down the hill and gathered at the meeting hall. Food and cake had been collected beforehand from each family. My mamah had already pounded the brown rice and the white rice in the rice pounder and made flour and delicious cakes with palm sugar and coconut milk and fragrant pandanus leaves. She wrapped her cakes in banana leaves and steamed them. She put them aside for the party in the meeting hall and then made *wajik*, a traditional cake from her own tribe. It was steamed brown rice mixed with palm sugar and pressed hard in a tin tray to make it solid before cutting it. The people in the village would make sango, the traditional cake from brown rice flour mixed with sugar or crushed banana, then fried. People who didn't have brown rice only made fried crushed cassava instead or brought nothing.

When we started the party, people sat down on the grass mats on the floor. In front of us were two men from the town demonstrating magic tricks. Once, after the magic, we saw a black and white movie on a fabric screen. It was the first time any of us had seen such a thing and many people came in from their ladangs just to see it. The movie had no story, only about a man burning garbage in his yard. The screen was bluish with smoke and people around us were excited and commenting all the time. "Oh, he will burn the house!" one of our neighbours said nervously. Then the screen changed and showed armies demonstrating their capability in the field, jumping, crawling and rolling with guns in their hands. The movie was short. Some of the men lit kerosene lamps when it was about to end, but they shut them off to make the movie more visible.

Afterwards it was time for the cakes. The women went up to the table in the front of the room, picked up the cakes and divided them. Once, one of our neighbours named Indai Ungking went up and took my mamah's cake and replaced it with hers. My mamah was complaining, saying that the woman was terrible because she didn't even share it with other people, but took it all home. Early in the party, Indai Ungking had already put her eyes on the cake, which was famous, but she pretended not to see Mamah's eyes. She was a midwife in our village and her husband was a retired teacher, an old cheerful man who always talked Dutch. He loved *tuak*, the rice wine, and never left any behind.

During my childhood, Indai Ungking and her husband were our neighbours and she came many times to our house day and night. She sometimes went home happily with some seasoning or salt my mamah gave to her. One morning I went to the kitchen early to watch my mamah cooking and Indai Ungking was already there visiting. We always had steamed rice with boiled vegetables or salty fish or sometimes boiled eggs picked from the special basket my papah made for our chicken to lay eggs in. Indai Ungking watched my mamah peel an onion and asked Mamah if she could have the onion skin. "For making *ragi*," she said, while she crushed and pressed it in her skinny hand. Ragi is the fermented rice flour that we need to make rice wine. You can mix pepper or even onion skin in it and make the rice wine as you want it — sour, sweet or bitter. Some people like bitter rice wine but women like it better sweet. For sour wine, we put salt in it.

Indai Ungking was an important midwife before the flying nurse came. My sister Yayang was born in her hand. When I came up after my marriage, she was also the one taking care of my pregnancy. She used to ask me to lie down on a grass mat and she rubbed coconut oil mixed with crushed onion on my stomach, then started pinching and pressing. It would sometimes feel so painful that I would ask her not to press so hard. I worried that she might hurt my baby. "I have to put the baby back in its position," she said innocently. She and her husband were very poor, and their farming was never enough because they had many kids to feed. Still they managed to send two of their children to be teachers in the town down the river. What I remember most clearly is how Indai Ungking loved the coffee my mamah made for her. She always said, "Hahapan . . . hahapan," to express how good it tasted, shaking the drops out until there would be nothing left in the glass. Many people in the village had coffee, but they didn't have real sugar. They made sugar from palm or from sugar-cane trunks which they squeezed until the juice drained out.

Some village ceremonies can take place any time. Whenever a visitor comes, for example. *Totak garung pantang* is a gate made of garung wood with lovely painting on it. Before a guest enters the village, he should stop at the gate and start a dialogue with the chief. The chief will ask his purpose and the guest will answer. They will talk before the gate is cut with a mandau—a sword. The chief will offer rice wine and they will drink together with a little music and dancing. This welcome ceremony is mostly arranged for government officials. When we have the *ikat tongang* ceremony with music and rice wine, a visitor is invited to sit on the gong and the chief will sprinkle rice on his head for prosperity. The visitor must lick the blade of a knife as a power symbol and rub himself with chicken's blood for strong spirit while muttering a mantra. Then he will get a tongang bracelet to wish him a safe journey and keep bad spirits away.

Tongang is a root that twists live on a tree trunk we use for the bracelets, to show deep feeling, to welcome guests and to cure the sick. In the ikat tongang ceremony we use the root, sangkuba leaves, rice, chicken blood and an iron knife.

Tongang symbolizes strong muscle or tendons.

Sangkuba leaves symbolize the strong and tireless body.

The iron knife is a symbol of strong spirit, like steel.

Rice is for prosperity.

For us, all these things have meaning.

3

Guru

I ENTERED SCHOOL IN the first grade and I wasn't smart because I couldn't read. I could count a little bit but not more. We met with our teacher a few times during the week but he never showed up if it was the season for making a new ladang. He spent most of his time cutting, burning and planting. He came back when the rice started to grow. At harvest time we would not see him at all. He disappeared in the ladang, sometimes for weeks. Ninety per cent of the students disappeared too, helping their parents in their ladangs.

There were thirty or forty students in our class. Some of them had very bad skin diseases and they were smelly like fish. This kind of skin disease was contagious. I was friends with the children of one family who lived close to our house. Their parents spent most of their time on the ladang. They would be gone for weeks guarding it from wild boar and deer and the children had to stay in the village to attend school. They were poor. My mamah sometimes warned me not to get too close to them because they suffered from skin disease and I had to be careful. But I did not care about my mother's warning.

One of the boys in that family was named Anjing, which means "Dog." It's normal for Dayak to pick an animal name for their children. There were fish names, plant names and animal names such as Gajah (elephant), Kaho (red ant), Keledai (donkey), or Padi (rice) and so on. We live close with nature and we believe that we are part of it.

So one day I got itchy on my upper arm and I kept scratching and a couple of days later I found a scaling spot that was as big as a coin. Of course I was terrified and tried to hide the spot from my parents. When I woke in the morning I ran to the backyard where we had a small garden and picked a cassava stalk and squeezed the sap and rubbed it on my spot. It dried quickly and I peeled off the skin. I did it many times. The skin sometimes bled and hurt but I had to cure the spot without my parents knowing about it. Luckily, my mamah had sulphur soap — a very good soap for killing bacteria. It was expensive and we had to buy it in the town. When I bathed in the river, I rubbed the soap on my spot desparately until it hurt. Gradually, the spot faded and was gone.

A girl named Mari who lived down the hill near the football field had scabies which spread over her whole body. Her skin was scaly and fishy and she was very vulnerable to the sun. If she got hot she would scratch her body badly and the skin would often bleed. She suffered so much from her disease that she always hid from meeting people. Everybody kept distant. But a German pastor brought pills and cream for her and patiently treated her and gradually her disease went away, and the boys who had insulted her and kept their distance from her before began to put their eyes on her. They called her Kembang Dukuh (plantation flower). Everybody tried to take her heart and wanted to pick the flower.

But the worst story is this: in our class there was a little girl, not so young any more to be in the first grade. She was stupid they said, so she was always in the same class. She was big and they said she did not have a really right mind. And sometimes she didn't take a bath for a week. This girl smelled and her hair was full of lice. Our headmaster asked her many times to wash her hair and clean it up but she didn't do it. So one day on a cloudy morning our headmaster suddenly came to class with scissors in his hand. He went directly to the girl, whose name was Ligi, and cut her hair. We saw hair everywhere. Then we saw her stand up at her desk and look shyly at all of us with tears and sad crying. Ligi was bald. The headmaster asker her to go home.

I got very scared. I was trembling at my desk and could not say anything and I wanted to cry and call my mother who was also a teacher in our school. I was afraid the headmaster might come to my desk and cut all my hair, which was long to my shoulders. My heart pounded. Many years later, when I met Ligi in my village, I was surprised. She was beautiful and had light skin and it was very soft but she was not married.

Often, some women came to our house to sell salty durian in bamboo cylinders. They came from a far away village called

Lopus by walking through the jungle and they wanted to barter for soap and salt. My mamah could not refuse as they had such a long walk. She bought the durian but we didn't use it because the sellers were obviously suffering from contagious skin diseases. My mamah never liked to buy salty durian from the villagers because she was not sure about the cleanliness. We liked to make it ourselves.

School was only about two hundred metres from our house. We could hear the iron bell and as soon as I saw the long row of children in front of each class I just ran without shoes and joined them. Many of my classmates came from another village. Early in the morning they had already walked on a small path to attend school. Some also came from the ladangs where they were helping their parents. One of my friends stayed with her parents on the ladang. After school finished at twelve she would change her clothes and pack them in her woven bamboo backpack and rush back to the ladang, five kilometres away. Sometimes she asked me to join her and said we could harvest cucumber and watermelon in her parents' ladang and I could get as much as I liked. I was eager but my parents said it was not safe to walk alone through the forest and you had to spend the night in the ladang because it would be too late to return the same day.

The elementary school was divided into six classrooms which had holes everywhere and dirty, spotted walls. A blackboard stood in front of each class, which contained fifteen desks in rows. Each held three students. I used to sit in the front desk which was very good because I could always hear the teacher clearly. But sometimes I was not so fond of the teacher talking so fast that his saliva poured like locat drizzling on our table, especially since our teacher had fake teeth! Sometimes I had to take refuge somewhere else to save myself.

For us, Saturday was the day we were really waiting for. We did not have to study that day and used to do some work like cleaning the class, sweeping the school yard or doing sports. Our favourite sport was called *kasti* ball, and is similar to cricket. We used a tennis ball, or a ball made from the sap of rubber trees, and hit it by turns with a stick and ran as fast as we could before the other team got the ball and hit us with it. We had to reach the pole on the other side of the field. I was good because I could run quite fast and nimbly to avoid the ball, but when I got hit . . . ugh. It hurt like burning on the skin. When we knew that our points were higher than the other team's, all the pain and hurting was as if washed away.

On the special day when we moved up a grade everybody tried to bring the nicest and most delicious food or cake. They divided it in half and gave half away to the teacher and the rest they could share with the class.

After the party, everybody cleaned up and then waited nervously for the reports. In my class I used to be the one who did work like writing the subject of the lesson on the blackboard which my friends would re-write it in their books, so I did not really feel nervous. But some students were pale and almost cried. The teachers called the names and handed out the reports and the students who passed had to leave the room and rush to the next class, screaming and joyfully trying to choose the best desk. The happy screaming was broken by the sound of crying. The ones who had not got called had to stay in the same class for another year. And their embarrassed and sad faces coloured the air.

The students called my mother "guru." This means teacher — a very respected person — a person people come to for help and advice. My mother used to tell us about one of her naughty students. This student used to sit next to the window and if someone passed, especially a girl, he would spit at her and of course the girl would scream because her clothes or hair would be spotted by spittle. My mother would get angry and come after the student with a wooden ruler. But as soon as the student saw my mother coming, he'd stand up and jump out the window. It was two and a half metres from the ground, but he always managed very well.

One day I met this young boy as a grown-up man with a wife and some children. He was handsome and chewing betel nut all the time. He and Mamah shared old stories about the time he was still her student and they were laughing a lot remembering.

In the afternoon Mamah would ask some of her girl students to make flour from our rice. They would pound and grate the rice in the mortar and she'd give them some little present to take home like salt or seasoning. These girls would be very happy to get the gift. My mother would mix the flour they had made with palm sugar and coconut milk and make cakes. They were good and sweet and I loved to take a few with me in my pocket to divide with my friends when I went outside to play. My friends were so grateful because many of them came from very poor families.

I loved to be in the kitchen when my mother was cooking. I sat on the rice bag watching and when I got bored I went to the corner next to the fire stove and picked up some bananas. I like a kind of banana we call rattan banana because of its shape. Sometimes I'd play with the *kisaran* — a piece of equipment for grating rice. We would put rice in it and grind chum-chum and from the little space in the middle of the grinder the white rice would fall down. I liked to play with it and watch the rice peel off its skin and fall down white and fragrant on the grass mat.

One morning, I got my own breakfast and sat on the floor to enjoy my rice. I love our rice because it's very fragrant, especially fresh from the new harvest. I ate with my brothers and sisters. I was supposed to go to school and I didn't know why I didn't go until I remembered that my mother was giving birth. It was a cloudy morning and some people were busy helping and one of the other women went inside and out from bedroom to kitchen always carrying something in her hand that I didn't recognize. What was it for? My sisters were wandering around in the sitting room because the women asked us not to go in and I heard my mother's soft groaning and finally a strange crying. A baby. My sister.

Later, when my mother took the baby she held her to her chest with a long cloth tied on her shoulder. Suddenly she said something. "Putrisia." I looked at her but I didn't understand. Then I knew that she had found a name for my new sister. That was the name. The baby was very beautiful and had a light skin. Everybody loved her. One Sunday morning my mother dressed us all up. We walked up the village to the church which was standing on the hill. The church my grandfather built. It was a small church built of wood. I was sitting in front and I saw the priest baptise my little sister. I heard him spell something and say the name of Christ and name my baby sister. The name was beautiful. Putrisia Astari, but she is called Yayang. My mamah did not want to follow Dayak style of naming because we are usually named after a plant or an animal; also trees, fish, even hard material such as *meja* (table), *piring* (plate), and so forth.

When I was young my mother and father called me with the endearing name Isa although I didn't like that name because of the other name of the Christ (Isa Almasih). I was scared. I felt guilty because in Dayak culture we believe if we use the name of Allah, we will get cursed. We are not able to carry the name because it is too heavy, too glorious, so we can get sick, like the boy in a small village far away on the left river. He was named Allah because the parents wished him to be gorgeous like Allah, but he got sick all the time and almost died. Then his parents brought him to a medicine man. They made a ceremony for him. They gave him a mantra. And the medicine man asked the parents to change the boy's name. A name like Allah, that's forbidden, he said. The parents changed the boy's name and the boy survived and gained good health after the ceremony. I asked my mamah about it, but it was not easy to change my name.

When my friends heard my mamah call me Isa, they turned it to Kalingkasa, which is a fresh water fish's name. I hated that and I started finding names to call them to match. We had a boy living with us whose father's name was Taman, which means "garden" and his mother's name was Padi, which means "rice." I teased him and put it together to be Rice in the Garden. And another boy had a father named Motor (engine) and his mother's name was Meja (table). I combined it to be Engine on the Table and the boy was really angry as it is very taboo to say a parent's name among Dayak people, but I pretended to be talking about something else.

Finally when I was in senior high school I asked my parents' agreement to insert one L in front of Isa, and I became Lisa. Even though this was not a common name for a Dayak, since Christianity came, many of us are familiar with some western-style names. I used that name during high school and I was happy with it.

But my real name, Antariksawan, was given to me by my grandfather in regards to the Apollo spacecraft which landed on the moon in 1969. Antariksawan means Astronaut. When I entered school, my mamah changed it to be Riksa Orpa Sari because she thought Astronaut meant a man. She took half the name and put Sari behind it which means essence. When I started to become a guide, some of my new friends from Kumai had trouble with my name because their teeth are not complete. They have problems from drinking water or brushing their teeth with salty water because it lacks phosphorous, so they lose their teeth early. Anyway, they called me Riska and I have used that name ever since.

4

We Forgot about Danger

"ISAI BULI! COME HOME! I heard my mamah screaming from the house. I'd been playing outside since noon and she always called me home in the late afternoon. Sometimes she got angry if I took my little sister Lilis playing too far away. She worried that maybe I would take her to the river, which was deep and fast. But that afternoon I had asked my sister to play in the schoolyard, less than half a kilometre from our house. We were playing a game called *culupan* with Bongu, my close friend. We had decided on a pole which we had to step over. The rules were simple. We decided who would be the one chasing. We called her "chaser." She had to chase the "runner" and touch her before the runner got to the pole, where she could rescue herself.

So the point of this game was: the fastest one is the winner. We would run and the chaser tried hard to get us before we touched the pole. If she got us first, we had to play chaser. It was back and forth. Mostly we played this with a big team up to five, but at the moment we were only three. Then, in the middle of the game my sister fell down and hurt her upper lip. She was weeping and we lifted her up from the ground. I was nervous that our mother would find out so we tried to comfort her and I carried her on my back. And I was right. Our mother pulled my ears very hard as punishment.

The name of my friend, Bongu, means Ground Frog. I remember that she was very dark as a child and wore torn clothes. I was never sure how she could be so sweet when she was grown up. She married a man from Madura, a small island near Java, and had two kids. She was still dark but she was very chubby and her skin was smooth and her features were more like an Indian girl. I heard gossip that she ran away from her husband because he found out that she had a relationship with her brother-in-law. Years later, when I came back to the village she came to our place asking for medicine for her baby. I couldn't hand her anything as the medicine we had was only for a different sickness. I was also thinking that the baby just had a little stomach problem but later on it was too late to save the baby. She passed away. I felt bad especially when the mother — my friend — came by some days afterwards. Her face was gloomy and her eyes were empty. She sat in front of the kitchen door, saying that now only one child was left and groaning about how lonely she felt. I felt guilty for not doing anything to save her little girl. Even though she did not really take care of her kids, at the time she was a mother who had lost one of them. Many months after I heard that she went down the river and back to her husband with the only child left.

I also had another good friend, whose father was rich and owned a big ladang. Her mother was a strange woman who did not like to be in public. She seldom came up to the village but stayed all the time on their ladang in the hut with the pigs. People were scared of her because they said she was one of the *abuhan*, a woman who has black magic and can take off her head after rubbing her neck with *minyak bintang*, star oil. The people in the village said that when the moon is dead she wandered around flying in the air looking for women giving birth, sucking the blood and eating the placenta. Her eyes were deep and wild and nobody liked to be around her. She kept to herself in the ladang all the time.

Once a brave Dayak man was sneaking under my friend's longhouse and waiting there. The moon was dead and the night was dead. Then the woman came home from looking after her bamboo fish traps in the river. She came into the house carrying the bamboo basket and the young man was still under the house. The woman sat down and ate her fish which were still alive. Krauk . . . krauk . . . the sound of her cip cap cut the air and the young man could not bear it any longer and ran back to the village.

In the morning Mamah would wake me up and together we would go down to the river. Mamah would carry her big plastic bucket to get clean drinking water. She wrapped a sarong around her body and carried her bucket along with soap. My mamah was beautiful and had long hair to her waist or even longer. She loved to knot it at her neck. Her skin was light and that made me wonder because my skin was not light except under my clothes. Sometimes my sister Ita would bathe with us.

Mamah had to teach her class and before that she had to prepare food for us. She would first light the fire in the fire stove with a little kerosene and some firewood. After that she would take one or two scoops of rice from the storage jar. She cleaned it in the cooking pot before setting it on the fire stove. It would take fifteen to twenty minutes to be done but before the water dried, she would scoop some of it out of the rice and give it to us to drink. It was creamy and fragrant. We loved to mix some sugar in to make it rich and delicious.

One morning I woke up early and I went to the kitchen to get my tea in a small tin cup, but when I passed the table I saw a big scaly animal underneath. It was dead. I saw the head with its little tongue showing. I was curious, so I pulled the tongue and it got longer and longer each time I pulled. I got nervous and guilty, feeling that my parents would find out what I'd done, so I tried to push the tongue back in the little mouth, but it did not go back. So I hurriedly moved away so nobody would find out that I'd been pulling the tongue. When I got breakfast, I pretended not to know anything and asked what the animal was. My mother said "It's *trenggiling*," an anteater, and asked me to finish my rice.

My older brothers, Eby and Uber, liked to go to the forest to trap birds. They made a snare with bamboo poles and grain. They often brought home some wild pigeons which they put in small wooden cages by the house. We ate the bird meat which we fried in coconut oil. But Mamah was not happy with that. She always worried every time her children went to the forest that we might be attacked by snakes or wild boar or even fall in the *balantik* trap that releases a deadly bamboo spear when you step on it. The trap is usually used for catching wild boar.

My brothers never brought swallows home as our parents warned us not to disturb them. Taboo, they told us many times. Swallows are a kind of bird who bring luck to us and my brothers never caught any as it might bring bad luck. In our house we had a swallows' nest by the window. My sister and I loved to see the chicks almost every morning. While waiting for our breakfast, we climbed the window and watched the little babies, not as big as our brother's toe, screeching and hungrily opening their small mouths everytime they saw our head poke through the window. Their mamah usually came in the afternoon with some grass with grain on it to feed her little hungry chicks while our mamah worried that if we stood by the window we could fall out, since our house was on high stilts.

In the cupboard in our living room, we kept a glass jar where my grandfather stored an embryo of a deer in arak. I sometimes squatted and watched it. The deer was wrinkled and soft with big, open eyes. He'd already been there for a long time. My grandfather drank the arak from the jar and my uncle too. They said it made you strong and young. I haven't seen my papah drink it. He did chew betel nut like most of the people in our village and in other Dayak places. He ate it after he mixed it with white paste made from burnt freshwater shells from the river and folded it inside the spicy betel leaf. It was like tooth paste. Then he would mix in some sap of the gambir tree or just the gambir leaves. The other stuff was *pinang*, areca fruit. He would chew the areca nut first, then chew the paste and gambir which was folded nicely in the betel leaves.

Most people, especially old people, chewed betel nut. Their teeth and mouth turned red and even black because they never brushed their teeth. But their teeth stayed strong and healthy from eating this stuff. My father's teeth were very strong, but he brushed them at least once a day. Mamah said betel nut made you look ugly with red and black teeth. It was making people addicted. They mostly did not smoke but they chewed a lot. Sometimes I tried chewing as well. But we had to make sure that nobody played with the areca fruit, such as throwing it in the air and catching it back and forth. If the nut was treated in such a way, it could produce a kind of result that made you really drunk and flying when you ate it. You felt chilled and light, very light. I felt this way once. I was standing and my body was so light I could not keep my balance and bumped into anything close to me.

We have special medicines for everything. Papaya root can be used to cure and prevent malaria or skin disease or even fever. We take the juice of the boiled haro root after giving birth. I used to climb this tree and eat the fruit when I was small. After giving birth it helped me recover. The bitter yellow stuff can fasten the abdomen muscle and a woman's secret part, which is ruined after giving birth.

One of the things I remember about our life in the village is my older brothers' circumcisions when they were twelve or thirteen. This kind of circumcision is very traditional. We use two pieces of bamboo that we make smooth. We stick them under the tip of the penis. The medicine man will pinch the skin on the tip, then wrap the bamboo with rattan so it's very tight. It's the outer skin that must come off. The bamboo can stay two weeks, sometimes one month, before it will be opened. Then when it's opened, the skin will drop off by itself. And it will recover, but it's very painful. Sometimes the boys get infections. I remember both my brothers crying in the night. They wore only loose sarongs. Almost every night they lay down over a basin of water and let their penises hang down and soak in the water to reduce the pain and swelling. Also before they insert the bamboo, they soak in the river for at least two hours in the dawn. At four o'clock in the morning they will get in the water and two hours later the medicine man will try to put the bamboo together. Finally, near the place where they pee, the skin will be rotten, because the bamboo is sharp, and then little by little it falls off.

Not so many people do this any more. We have doctors who do it without any pain at all. But some people who don't have any money, they still bring their children to a medicine man and ask for *sopitan*. Up the river for a doctor it's 25,000 or 30,000 rupiahs. Afterwards, we must give a little party.

One afternoon, when we still lived with my grandparents, I was playing games with my friends. We ran and chased each other not far from my house. One of my friends crashed into me while I was running and I could not save my balance. I fell down really hard on the ground and broke my right arm. I was crying because my hand was so painful when I tried to move it. My father wrapped my arm with woven bamboo to prevent the arm from being misshaped. I had that wrap for many weeks and I had to eat with my left hand. It was difficult. Sometimes in the morning I woke up very lonely and weeping because my hand was so painful and swollen and it hurt to move it. I had to walk like a robot, slowly and carefully. Everytime I made a sudden movement it brought so much pain. I remember I sat on the table next to my grandfather one misty morning and we ate together and I used my left hand and my grandfather looked at me and teased me. He said I used the same hand we used to do the washing after the toilet business. I couldn't say anything, otherwise my sister and brother would tease me the same way.

We had a middle-sized rice barn where we stored all our harvest. On the wall of the rice barn nested a bunch of wild bees. They could sting and we had to be careful when loading or storing the rice, otherwise they would feel disturbed and come after us. But we let them stay because our family believed that they brought luck to us. Indeed, our rice barn was always full and we were never starving when a scarcity came in the village. At a certain time we harvested the honey as well. Once, the man we had hired to get the honey was not feeling too daring because the bees were flying around noisily. Then my uncle Guyak, the younger brother of my papah, got an idea. He took the rice storage basket and covered himself with it. Head to thigh. As he stepped over and climbed the ladder to reach the beehive, the bees flew around noisily and then suddenly my uncle went running, tumbling over and shaking his basket, screeching. Everybody was laughing at him as he fought off the bees who had sneaked inside the basket. He was swollen all over.

That day they finally managed to get the hive and I got a big piece of it with the larva still inside. It was fun when I opened the layer which covered the holes, pinched the heads of the larva and ate them fresh. They were sweet and very fat and felt warm in the stomach. We squeezed the rest of the hive and drained out the honey.

My older sister Ita (Arita) once had a problem with *amandel*, or tonsilitis. Her tonsils were swollen and she had difficulty eating because it was painful to swallow anything. Her tonsils were getting worse but she did not want an operation on them. She was too scared even to hear the word. My parents asked her to try a traditional way. Next to the house where we lived then (in the factory compound at Pangkalan Bun) we had a fishpond and there was a small tree of seloban. It was a young tree, its trunk not even bigger than my mother's arm. She told my sister to peel off the bark and boil it. She had to drink the juice daily. My sister was in junior high school then and she was a grown-up girl already. So she peeled off the bark everyday and drank the juice for about two weeks and until now she has never had an operation and her tonsilitis disappeared.

When I was in the fifth grade of elementary school, I fell ill from *sakit kuning*, or hepatitis. My body was turning yellow all over. My eyes, my skin, even my urine was completely yellow. I had to lie down for three months and my stomach and liver were badly swollen. Every time I breathed, my chest was painful. Everyday my mom would cook me rice cereal and mix it with spinach.

I could eat eggs but not fried food or meat. My parents also asked me to eat glasses of plain sugar every day. My illness was getting worse and I had to move slowly just to go pee. My mamah searched for *akar kuning*, the traditional medicine we used to cure hepatitis. She finally got it from her friend, the root of the akar kuning tree which grew in the forest. She boiled it and asked me to drink the yellow, bitter juice every day as much as I could take. Not long after, my illness got better and soon I attended school again.

I used to swim with friends in the rapids in our village and get bruises on my feet because I grazed them on sharp rocks. Sometimes we went to the jungle looking for firewood; sometimes we climbed trees trying to find wild fruit. I loved to eat a kind of small fruit we call *karamunting kodok*. These are small blue berries we could find easily.

When my friends and I went to the forest to play, looking for wild fruit or climbing trees, we forgot about danger.

I used to climb my favourite jambu fruit tree. I claimed it was mine and made my sister Lilis ask my permission to climb it. I could spend many hours up there just sitting. And once I climbed the rambutan tree and almost fell five or six metres because the trunk was slippery. With a beating heart I had to crawl down. I didn't want to explain that the cause of the markings on my skin was the rambutan tree. I kept this as my secret because if my papah knew he would beat me with the rattan he always kept in the cupboard, ready for us. If he beat me with that it often left a long red mark for days and hurt very much. One time, he found out I was climbing the coconut tree by the river and pulling down all the coconuts I could reach. I hid them under the tree covered with leaves and even though I said I didn't do it, he beat me badly. Later I found out he knew by the coconut fibres on my clothes and in my hair. He said it was better for him to beat me than to see me break my bones. It was very painful. Oh, I cried like hell! My father was very strict with my older brothers too, but I wish that he'd taken the rattan to my younger brother. Then things might have been different for us when we grew up.

My friends and I used to go across the river by dugout canoe to collect dead branches. We went across the river because in my grandpa's ladang the dead wood was plenty. We cut the branches into short small pieces, loaded our firewood neatly in the canoe and carried it on our backs to the village. My mamah always worried if she found out. She said it was dangerous in case of a snake attack or sudden flood. She also told me that as a daughter of a respected teacher in the village I should not go around looking for firewood. But I insisted and sneaked out with my friends. I think I was a little bit naughty before, as a child.

When I looked for fruit with my friends we went to the forest and played there for half the day, then went to the river to swim. We played a game that we called *ilung*. One of us would hide a stone wrapped in ilung leaves in the deep of the river bottom. The others would search the bottom of the river. I was very good sometimes. I would dive and put the stone among the grasses so it wasn't easy for my friends to find. Mostly they would try several dives and come up out of breath. It was a fun game because the water was so clean with small stones and a sandy bottom and it was only one or two metres deep. After we were satisfied with this game we would get out of the water pale and cold and dry off quickly and run to the village for other games.

Another thing to do was to collect fresh rubber to make a ball. My brother would tap the rubber trunk, circling it with a knife, and collect the fresh streaming sap in a small bamboo container. It wouldn't be much and we had to keep making new taps and putting the container under them. Usually we tapped them in the afternoon and in the morning my brother would collect the fresh sap and bring it home. He would place a flat plank by the sand and lay the sap thickly on the plank. He'd wait till the sap dried a bit and then roll a small round stone over it. He sometimes let me roll the stone over and over until it was covered by thick layers of sap and shaped like a ball. The ball was hard and elastic and we used it to play kasti. If one of us went home crying with too many bruises from the ball, we'd soon hear a mother's angry sound from the distance. We'd scatter and run home nervously before the angry mother came to the school field where we were playing.

One day I was playing in the river with some friends and suddenly we heard a strange sound. Something moved. The leaves moved, and we heard somebody make a sound from the leaves, a very high-pitched sound. Suddenly all the people in the river shouted, *"Ngayau! Ngayau!"* They grabbed all the other children and ran and I was left alone. I didn't know why. I tried to see across the river but there was only the sound in the leaves. I was alone and afraid, but one of the village men came back, grabbed me by the hand and helped me run away. I didn't see anyone across the river, but I heard the sound, and I saw some movement. Then the old people told us what happened. *Ngayau* means headhunter.

Headhunters had come to our area to find heads for the burial ceremony. They need these human heads to accompany the soul to heaven. Our longhouses have ladders leading to the door because of problems with these headhunters. At night we pulled the ladder inside the house so no one could get in, and then we put it down again in the morning.

Mostly they chop off the head, put the head in a rattan backpack and leave the body. Headhunting is now forbidden, of course. Our government asks us not to do it. So our people don't use human heads any more. Not legally. They use cow heads or buffalo heads. They try to do their ceremonies that way. But in fact the original practice still exists.

Dayak children are sometimes kidnapped for this reason. And there are still raids.

When I was in high school, in a village up the river an old man asked his grandson to get a head for him when he died. Finally the grandfather died. As the boy wanted to show his respect, his devotion to the older people of his family, he was trying to do what his grandfather asked. The funeral was getting closer and closer and he asked his girlfriend to go to the forest with him. For a picnic.

His girlfriend took another girl along with her. They went to the jungle, and there they found two men waiting. Those two men told the boy's girlfriend to lie down on a hollow tree, and they cut off her head. Her boyfriend did nothing, he was just looking. The other girl was really terrified and ran. They tried to catch her also, but she managed to escape. She ran back to the village and went to the police and told them what happened. She told the people. She was almost crazy from the sight. The police came to the place and found the body without a head. They arrested the young man who had asked the two men to behead his girlfriend. They sentenced him to a whole life in jail. The police took him because there was a witness — the other girl. She was almost crazy, really, but she was a witness who made our government and the police finally know about this kind of criminal. Before, when the people did headhunting, nobody ever knew about it. They never arrested anybody. They didn't know who did it. It just happened.

Near another village there was a band of headhunters and the people were afraid to go to their ladangs until one man, my friend's grandfather, went to the jungle and found a big longhouse. He and his friends waited until night and then — at midnight — they climbed up to the door of the longhouse and saw five heads, already smoked to keep them from rotting. They also saw about thirty headhunters asleep on the floor and one of them — the leader — was sleeping close to the door. So quickly my friend's grandfather killed him. He put the lamps out in the longhouse — mostly we have lamps that are close to the door — and after he killed the leader he jumped to the ground and waited. Finally the headhunters realized their leader was killed and began fighting with each other because they thought one of them had done it. They were fighting and one by one they fell to the ground and the village men, waiting below, just cut off their heads until there were no headhunters left.

Some headhunters eat seven leeches alive. It's a special kind of leech with a stripe on the back and when they eat seven of them alive they don't recognize their families any more and they have the strong desire to kill. We have many kinds of Dayak tribes and each one has its special way. Because my friend's grandfather always went after headhunters, some of the villagers believed that he was one himself. In some villages headhunting was the way a young man showed that he was brave. Sometimes no one knew which men were the headhunters. The ones who were killed by my friend's grandfather came from his own village. Two of this friend's brothers were almost taken! They'd all gone to the ladang with some of her friends and when she was busy picking cucumbers she heard a sound made from sucking on grass. It's a strange sound that warns people because head-hunters split up and they make this sound to signal each other. When she heard it she begged everyone to run because they might be attacked, but nobody listened. They said, "Oh, no, it's impossible." And she couldn't force them so she stayed with them.

She was still picking cucumbers when she saw several men coming from the other side of the ladang. The others — her friends — when they saw them, began to run and she followed. She ran and ran to save her life. But when she was a little further away, she remembered her brothers and ran back to find them. The men had already surrounded the boys, but headhunters have certain qualifications for their victims, so they were measuring them before they killed them.

My friend grabbed her two brothers and held onto them, all the time crying and shouting, "Don't take my brothers, don't take my brothers!" And the men finally turned away.

When she brought her brothers back to the village and told her family what had happened, her father and her grand-father chased after the men, but couldn't find them. They went back to the village and stayed under the longhouse to make sure everyone inside was safe. At that time all the villagers were scared. It was only about eleven or twelve years ago. Very recently.

We still have lots of headhunters; but now maybe people don't know the sound they make because we never hear it. A woman in Kumai was going with her boyfriend to a small neighbouring town. We didn't have any roads there yet. You had to go along a small path through the jungle, and it was two days' walk. They kept walking and walking. In the middle of the night her boyfriend said to her that he wanted to get a light to smoke a cigarette. He said she'd better wait there and he would find a place with a light.

She waited, but he didn't come for a long time. She got scared and tried to find him. She walked without light in the middle of the night in the jungle. Finally she came to a small hut and heard her boyfriend's voice. He seemed to be calling her. She was scared but she went inside. There were no lights but she managed to get in and she touched something wet and found out it was blood. She had touched a hanging body. Without a head.

Then her boyfriend's voice came closer and closer and she realized he wasn't normal. He had said he wanted to get a light in the middle of the night in the jungle. And how had he found this place so easily? She slipped out behind the house and ran and ran and ran.

5

The Last Day
Meeting

ONE DAY WE CHILDREN were watching a *bukung*
dance when some old women called us to come to
them. A line of people were carrying a coffin to the burial
ground and a woman was sitting on it with a long knife,
samurai-like in her right hand, raised up against the sky. I saw
my best friend's father dancing so beautifully in front of the
house wearing his *luha*, a painted mask and shaking a bamboo
stick to produce a harmonic sound. In his left hand was a
handkerchief and sometimes he bowed almost to the ground
then jerked back up rapidly. The air was full of magic and
tears and glory and the old women put crushed saffron on my
head to protect me from the bad spirits so they would not
steal my soul.

After somebody dies, two men have the job of telling all of the people in the village about the dead person. They go around the village, bringing a spear, and they cry and scream and after people come, they start to make the wooden coffin from a round log. Sometimes it takes one or two days to finish it. After we bathe the corpse, we do the *pamo*. It's a ceremony where we put the corpse in the coffin along with many valued things like coins, old jars or antique plates. But we must break these things first, because if we break them they will be fine again and even more lovely in heaven. All of these things are for the dead person so he will not be poor in heaven.

After bathing the dead person, we put clothes on him. While we are doing this, the music is playing — music we call *tipa bamba*, which is a special kind of music for the dying ceremony. There are several kind of gongs and tambourines. We put the wooden coffin in the middle of the room, in the longhouse. We direct the feet of the corpse towards the door. Sometimes we let the dead person stay in the coffin for one week, sometimes for several months — it depends who it is. If the person is very high in our village, we keep him longer in the house. And sometimes we have to keep the body waiting for the relatives to come. We have our own way to preserve the body. We use a big, round log of ironwood from the jungle for the coffin. Then we seal it with rubber. After seven days we make a hole under the coffin and we put a bamboo cylinder down to the ground to drain the liquid away. We close the hole and make a fence around it so a pig doesn't come and dig.

So, the old women who put crushed saffron on our heads to protect our souls from bad spirits, led us into the longhouse to look at the decorated coffin, and we saw paintings on it made from *kasumba*, a small tree that produces a very red colour from its seeds. The black colour is from the wood we burn.

This was my first dying ceremony.

People came to see the body before it was sealed in the coffin, bringing rice wine or rice or chicken or pigs and we watched them come in. Some volunteers were doing all the work. One group went to the jungle to find firewood, collect wild vegetables, wild bamboo shoots. The funeral would take a long time and they had to feed all the people who were going to come. A second group made rice wine and another prepared everything else they would need for the ceremony.

The next thing that happened was that people started to imitate evil behaviour or terrible animals but still in a polite way. They wore loincloths and covered their bodies with clay. They painted their faces like animals and danced because they wanted to call the evil spirits in from outside. When a person dies, many bad spirits come around. The dancers have beautiful masks, very big — sometimes as much as a metre in diameter. They put them on and dance so the bad spirits will come, imitating them and scaring children, covering themselves with clay, with masks, making jokes, behaving like monkeys to amuse people, the family. One mask was like a big butterfly, beautiful. Another mask was like a parrot, another a monkey, another like a dragon. Some people can make them very well and when somebody dies, and the chief asks the men to dance, if they have a mask they can join in.

We children were growing tired, but that night there was the ceremony called *malam marindui*. It means "the last day meeting," and for this there is a miniature house made of bamboo filled with cakes, vegetables, spices, rice, meat or rice wine. This house, called *balai padaro*, provides the dead person with supplies. But first, when they came to the house, each woman went to the wooden coffin and cried. It was a kind of crying we call *kumang rawa* — to escort the soul to heaven. The women must cry beside the coffin and when they cry, it's just like song. Sometimes while crying they talk about how good this person was, about how kind he was before, when he was alive. They give their sympathy but it's a little bit scary to hear how they cry. They really cry, then they stop, and then they're crying again. I don't know how they manage. When they cry it's so the people will not feel so bad. All night we could hear the women crying accompanied with a special rhythm of *batipa*. In the morning, the bukung was danced again, with good clothes, and they used the masks, the luha. They danced outside with *tipa* music. They shook bamboo and it produced a nice sound.

Many years after that funeral my mamah told me the dead man's story. His wife, named Kaus (sock), was young and beautiful and another man fell in love with her and slept with her, but the husband found out and chased after the man, fought and killed him. Some armies came after the husband and he ran to West Kalimantan crossing the jungle and spending most of his time hiding. The armies had orders to get him dead or alive. One day they found him sitting in a hut in front of the firestove cooking and the armies rained bullets on him and he fell to the ground in his own blood.

The burial ceremony I witnessed was his. Nowadays, the wife who brought death on her husband still lives in the village. Her beauty is faded. Her teeth are black from chewing betel nut. Her beauty that once turned over men's hearts is now gone with time. And her husband is in his painted coffin . . . I remember lots of people joined together to escort that procession. You could hear the noise from the women who cry and cry. Then the coffin was put in a hole in the ground.

Over the grave mostly we put on one *tabak*, a kind of box made from ironwood. Depending how important the person is, we may add one or two or three more levels. Sometimes we paint it really nicely. We have two kinds of designs with a certain meaning. There is a long square we call tabak and another design like a sailing boat we call *lancang*. Then we make a structure, and inside, we keep several small statues. These are like bodyguards. Over the foot of the coffin, we give some motif, like a kind of animal, painted or carved and in the middle we give a kind of carving we call *akardalola* in several colours, red, black, white.

After the burial ceremony, everybody goes back to the house — where they kept the body before — and they'll have music again. Once again, the owner must feed all the people who attend the ceremony. After they finish eating, if there's something left, they supply it to everybody who wants it. Sometimes there's lots of food, and they take it away so there's nothing left in the house. They can't keep the food in the house after they bury the dead body because the food is now dirty for the people who are in mourning, and they must take it away so everything is clean in the house.

After about forty days, if this person left a wife, she must do a little ceremony — a little music, a party. The medicine man comes to her to do a little ceremony to release her from the soul of the dead person. Near my village we have the mountain we call Sabayan. It's the place where Sanghyang Duato, our highest god, lives. Mount Sabayan is covered with flowers and clouds and at noon we can sometimes hear a chicken screaming from the mountain and we believe it's not a chicken but a spirit who makes the sound. If we go up there we ask for protection because we believe the place is holy; if we must climb the peak for some reason, if we see something strange, we should not say, "Oh, what is it?" We must be quiet.

In our village many people were Christianized by the pastor who came many times from down the river. He was from Germany. His skin was very pale and his nose was long. He was very tall, also. To the villagers, he was very strange, so all eyes fixed on him. Many villagers came from their ladangs just to see what he looked like. Some old people had only seen white people a long time ago during the colonial period. Our original religion was Kaharingan. It was animism and similar to Hindu. We have many gods. Good and bad spirits. Mount Sabayan is always covered by a mysterious fog. Our heaven is there, called *Surugo Dalam* (Deep Heaven), the place where we will go when we die. Many people have tried to go there for good luck, but nobody arrives even at a foothill if they're not blessed. If somebody wants to go there, they have to fast and clean themselves, be blessed by a medicine man and have a certain ceremony. The wood-seekers and woodcutters used to do this for good luck. If they were not clean when they came to this mountain, they would not find the wood they were looking for even though they searched everywhere. Many stories are told about how they found the beautiful old *garu* wood (alloeswood) on Sabayan but when they went back to harvest it, the tree was mysteriously gone. Garu or *gaharu* (in Bahasa Indonesia) is a very expensive item. Chinese like it for incense and medicine. We use it with our offerings. My mamah used to read us the story of poor Maria Magdelena, who rubbed Jesus' feet with expensive fragrant oil. The fragrance means something good. Dayak gods also loved it, but we didn't always use it because it was difficult to get. The wood collectors had to go deep in the jungle and spend many weeks to find the wood. If they were lucky, they could harvest some kilos of alloeswood, which would make good money for them.

Sometime after the burial party, we make the *ayahan* to take the soul off, so the spirit will not stay around the family, and to clean and wipe all the mistakes off between the dead and the rest of his family. In this ceremony, we open the grave and take the bones and clean them, then we put the bones in a small structure we call *sandung*. But not everyone can do it because it requires lots of money. So there are two kinds of ayahan. The first happens after a few years: we dig out the body, clean the bones off, and put them in a sandung. When we have enough money we do it the other way, we make the dying ceremony and the ayahan ceremony at the same time. In this case, we don't have to dig out the body. We do symbolic ayahan in the grave. But the other takes some time to wait for the body, to let it rot in earth so we can clean it. The older people in the family, they help. The sandung — it's a small building — like a house, with a floor, and they can keep the body in it. They clean the bones and put them in an antique jar from China or Burma. The Dayak here don't know how to make these jars. They put the jar in the sandung and the dead person goes safely to heaven.

Finally, we put up a big pole to remember the person. The poles are about five to ten metres high, made of iron-wood. We dig a hole, then give offerings in it, like eggs, rice wine. . . We believe that the god of the Earth will take this offering. After that ceremony we erect the pole. Sometimes we put it in front of the house, or some place near the buried body. If the person who died is a very important person in the village, we will put several Chinese jars on the top of the pole. We make a hole in the jar, and put the jar on the pole. If the dead person is very wealthy, the family will put more jars. They just like to show people what they have. There's another thing that's special. It's an ironwood carving. The people make it to guard the dead. Sometimes we just put it in the graveyard. It depends.

So that's what happens when someone dies in the village.

6

Nothing Was Ever
the Same

FOR FIFTEEN YEARS my family lived in the place where I was born. But my mother wished to leave because it was so remote and isolated from any other place and my two brothers had left to study in the town of Pangkalan Bun. My father did not agree with my mother's wish but she convinced him and they made the decision together to move. However, the government officer would not give her the official letter to move. Without the letter, my mother was not allowed to leave her teaching job. She could never escape the village.

The government didn't want to move her to another school because she was so good and had already stayed in the village a long time. But many years passed and finally one night I saw my parents packing their things — a few clothes, a mattress and pillow and some food. They told me that we were going down the river to visit my brothers. Then I saw a lot of people, friends of mine, my mother's and father's friends, my uncle escorting us to the river where we had our small boat. We loaded our things and I saw my mother's eyes red and some women crying. The air was sad. We got in our small boat, which is seven or eight metres long with no engine. Everybody was waving and that was the last I saw of my village for several years. I was eight years old.

My mother was worried about Eby and Uber, who were studying in Pangkalan Bun — many days away by boat at the end of the Delang River and further along the Lamandau River. They had been living in a government dormitory. It was a little bit horrible, but at least they had a place where they could sleep at night. They were in junior high school and sometimes they used to come up to visit us by *kelotok*, a long-boat with an engine. It's called kelotok because of the sound it produces, klotok ... klotok ... tok, from the engine. It was dangerous for them; they were very young — thirteen, four-teen. The journey was long and hard.

At the time, government employees in the district of West Kotawaringin, which included Kudangan, had to go to Pangkalan Bun to receive their salaries. When Uncle Ian from Sekombulan went down to Pangkalan Bun to sell cof-fee, cloves and rattan, my mother would ask him to pick up her money, but she never received it because my uncle used it for his own needs.

As I said, my papah did not want to move but he loves my mamah and understood that she'd had enough of the village.

We moved by small boat without any engine and had to paddle for many days carrying sacks of rice, cooking pans and the kepok mattresses for all five of us children. I remember they made a fence around the boat to prevent our falling into the river especially when we passed any rapids. It was dangerous because if the boat capsized or sank, all the children inside would be trapped alive. The boat had a roof made of palm thatch but from rain above or river below, it was full of water all the time so that the man who accompanied us had to dip water out constantly. He was a solid Dayak man from Lopus village, which is about four or five kilometres down river from our village. He was a cheerful man with lots of laughing. He ate a lot, too. He could finish two big plates of rice in one sitting. When we stopped to spend the night, we would cook rice in the big cooking pan. He loved salty fish. He would take one for himself and bake it in the wood coals. Then he would squat by the riverbank eating his rice with the salty fish in the tin plate. My mamah and the children would spend the night in the boat; the men searched for a good place to sleep on the sand where they would make a fire and spread their grass mats. We had to make fire, otherwise the mosquitos would be zooming all over us. In the boat, we used our mosquito net. The men would talk until late before falling asleep, but my papah never actually slept because he had to make sure everything was safe. The journey was long, especially for all the kids, so when we stopped at a village called Riam Panahan, I was excited because then I could move around.

We spent the night there in the house of one of my father's friends. For us the arrival of the darkness, no matter what time, is the time for bed. My papah brought the mattresses and pillows from the boat to the longhouse and we spread them on the floor and got ready to sleep, but the owner's wife told Mamah not to let us sleep with our feet towards the door. "Taboo," she said, "you will invite the bad spirits," so we had to sleep with our body crossing the longhouse towards the walls. Mamah put the mosquito net over us which was tight at each corner with a long line hung to the wall. She told us that bad spirits could not enter a mosquito net. She said that when we sleep our soul is very fragile but a net helps to protect us from somebody who intends to attack us with black magic. When I awoke in the middle of the night and found myself out of the net, I quickly rolled back inside. But for Delang people, it isn't common to use mosquito nets. We just lie on the floor on a thin grass mat and cover ourselves from feet to head with a long cloth.

Inside my net I remembered Saragih cave, which appeared because of a broken taboo. According to this story, in Bambulung village the chief made a big party and invited everyone to come. He was a good chief, this man. All the ladangs in his village produced well, and he had a beautiful daughter, a wife, and at the party there would be lots of amusement and food.

When the people arrived, the chief told them it would be taboo to utter a curse during the party. That was his rule. As I said, he had a lovely daughter. But this chief had a selfish wife. For a week the people enjoyed themselves, but the chief's wife found an excuse to stay in her room and never came out to greet her guests.

When the party was over, the chief entered his wife's room and found her with another man. Forgetting the taboo, he cursed her and suddenly thunder and hurricanes covered the village, and the house, the whole village, turned into a cave.

The cave is still looked after by an old man and it's possible to go inside, where you can hear someone crying. But never say anything bad in that cave or you won't find your way out.

One thing more. People in the area believe they can ask the help of the chief and his beautiful daughter if they are trying to find a husband or wife.

Maybe I dreamed about that cave, I don't know, but the next morning, I woke to the sound of chickens underneath the house. My mamah was busy with the owner in the kitchen at the back and the fragrance of rice filled the air. I went out and walked with my bare feet in the wet grass. There was some cow's dung there so I had to watch my step. The cows and pigs and chickens were roaming freely through the village so the villagers had to make sure their fences were strong enough to prevent the cows from entering their gardens and ladangs. I picked some wild flowers and had to jump to get them because they were higher than I was. I also went to the river and I saw the owner of the house coming down with her daughter who was the same age as me. The owner was wearing long cloths wrapped around her body. While she was washing in the river, suddenly she began screaming and grabbing her little daughter, who was almost taken by the water while she was playing. I heard her talking loud to her and I heard a buk . . . buk sound and the girl's screeching and crying. I did not dare to look closer and decided to move back to the longhouse. I did not say anything to my parents as they would be mad to know I was playing by the river.

We ate our breakfast, packed our things and continued our journey down river. Years later, I met the little girl who was almost taken by the water when she was studying in town to be an elementary school teacher. She told me that her boyfriend was waiting for her in her village. It's about one day's walk from my village to this Sekombulan village through the forest. She went back there after she graduated, full of dreaming, but when she got there her boyfriend was already married to another woman he had to marry because she was pregnant. My friend was so heartbroken and full of jealousy. She said that her parents were glad because they had never wanted her to marry him. After all, they were related and that is forbidden in the village and will bring bad luck. But she was jealous and vowed she would take him back for herself. She tried to get close to him and even though the wife was big with her pregnancy, she managed to get him back. People were talking about them, but she didn't care. People said the husband chose her because she got a job as a teacher which meant they would get a salary every month and a kind of prestige in the village.

They married as soon as the husband divorced his wife. The parents still did not agree to her marriage, but there was nothing they could do as their daughter was so stubborn. Not long after, she was pregnant but the baby was stillborn. When she lost her baby I was there in the village. She was groaning that she had been cursed, but one day I met her in the local market and she was carrying a new baby. When I wanted to see it, she hesitated but finally she let me see her baby. It was small and suffered from the hare-lip. The face was ugly because of the shape of the lips. The baby could not even close his mouth because his teeth were sticking out. All this happened later to that little girl who almost drowned.

We came down slowly, following the stream, passing small rapids and getting out of the boat when the rapids were big. We walked on the shore while my papah and the other man who accompanied us unloaded our things to lighten the boat. We walked to the end of the rapids then got in again when they managed to get the boat through the current. Many times we had to get out and walk because of so many dangerous rapids. I never suspected that our move would be permanent. Forever. My mamah told her headmaster, Guru Gansar, who was also my teacher, that we were only coming down to see my two brothers, Eby and Uber. But we never went back and the orders he sent to Mamah that she had to come back were ignored. "I gave him notice a long time ago and nobody cared," she said. So she started applying for jobs and got one in a small elementary school. She registered me in the second grade and my sister Lilis in the first grade and my older sister Ita in the fifth grade.

Pangkalan Bun is a small town with a mix of Malay, Javanese, Chinese and some native Dayak lucky to find jobs with the logging companies. Young Dayak students work part-time in the rows of Chinese shops by the edge of the main street or sell pork around town from pigs sent down by their families in the hinterland.

The town lies in the western part of Central Kalimantan and it was the capital of the ancient kingdom Kotawaringin, built almost five centuries ago. The Arut river cuts the town in two. One side is occupied mostly by Muslim people and the other side by groups of Chinese who build their family houses from dark ironwood — long, plain houses by the waterfront. The river is busy, with Malay boat-traders roaring by or tugboats struggling to pull long rafts of wood through the brown water.

In Pangkalan Bun Mamah had her job and Papah stayed because he loved her even though his heart was aching to go back to farming, hunting and tapping palm sugar.

In those days, in the beginning of our move from the village, everything was so difficult. My father was trying to earn some money by selling firewood. He would go to the lumber factory across the Arut River to get the leftover wood. With an axe he'd cut it into small pieces, nice pieces, and sell them. Every hundred pieces he sold for 250 rupiah. But when we had a flood, my papah could not sell wood because it was wet and took time to dry and because we did not have space to store it.

When we had a flood, even Mamah couldn't work. She would stay home with us because the water was high and Lilis and Yayang could not swim yet. We used a dugout canoe to get from the house to the street one hundred metres away. Many people drowned. Mamah told us that the water spirit.

Hantu Sungai, was looking for someone to be sacrificed because no one had fed him or given him regular offerings. Mamah told us that one of our neighbours went to the floating public public toilet in the middle of the night and saw a three-year-old boy on the dock staring quietly at the river. The old man shone his torch on the boy and asked him why he was there, but there was no answer so the old man felt uncomfortable and hoped the mother or father was inside the toilet since the river was flooding and would be dangerous. The child was naked, very dark and pygmy and ugly. When the old man started to ask something again, suddenly the child jumped into the river and disappeared under water. The old man shrank back. He waited a few moments, hoping the boy would come out, but nothing happened and he felt chilled. Without waiting any longer, he cancelled his urge to use the toilet and ran back home. "Hantu Sungai," he said. The spirit of the river. It was a bad omen.

Our small rented house was next to the Arut River and although it stood on stilts that were two metres high, in the rainy season the water often came over the floor and the air in the house was damp and cold. Papah then made a plank down the middle of the room like a temporary small bridge connecting the bedroom to the kitchen and living room. The water was as high as fifteen to twenty-five centimetres and could last for days, but with the plank laid higher than the water, we could walk on the plank and not get sick. Of course when Papah wasn't around, we jumped in the ankle high water and played. My brother sometimes made us a boat from paper. The paper boat would sink easily after it got wet but it was fun anyway. We even used our school paper to make the boat and sail it across the floor. When a real boat or speedboat outside on the river passed, the wave hit our floor and the wall and made a wave through the house.

At night, when there was a flood, we slept together in the only bed. It was too small for all of us and we had hardly any space to move or roll over. At night the air was terribly cold. The water was under our bed. The moisture dampened our clothes, the bed and the blanket. We were restless and we caught cold and coughed. Once my sister jumped from the bed in the morning and almost landed on the head of a long snake which crawled out from under the bed. It disappeared under the bed again before Papah could grab a stick. She was so upset she almost did not dare to put her feet down again. After that experience, my papah ordered some *kayu laki*, a long big root that has the function of preventing snakes from wandering around in the house. He ordered it from his friend in the Dayak village, who looked for it in the forest and sent it down to us. Mamah told me that the kayu laki scares snakes when they smell it. Papah stored it under the bed and we felt safe after that.

When he moved from Kudangan to the town down the river, I think some part of my father got left behind. But Mamah said spending fifteen years there was enough. She had gone to his village to teach and never complained. And she had to send her sons down the river to go to school past the sixth grade.

What I remember about Pangkalan Bun then is there were only one or two cars or a truck passing sometimes. The main street was empty and unpaved. My mamah wanted to settle there for the rest of her life. She did not want to go back to her family in Palangkaraya as she felt she did not belong there any more. Her parents said that they would give her a big piece of land for free if she moved to Palangkaraya, but she preferred to stay in Pangkalan Bun. She didn't want to leave her job. Sometimes I saw her sigh and gloomy and she would say that anyway she did not feel rooted and all the people she knew in Palangkaraya were not the same any more. When some years later she visited her own family, touched the ground after thirty years away, she found that everything had changed. She felt lost. My father felt uneasy because they still could not accept him because he came from Delang River, the place where many *kamuh* punishments are held. And we are born by that river too, and come from a father they call Orang Delang.

There is an old Dayak legend about two brothers. One of them, Bahai Jaro, is very poor. The other, named Bahai Dampu, is rich. One day Bahai Jaro asked his son to go to Bahai Dampu's house for some brown rice. All the rice in Bahai Dampu's house had been used for sango cakes but Bahai Dampu only gave his nephew some cakes made of wild rubber. When the boy went home he told Bahai Jaro that he had sango cakes but he couldn't chew them. He was hungry and there was nothing else to eat. Bahai Jaro was sad in his heart to know how his brother had treated his only son, giving him rubber cakes instead of a little food to eat, but the sadness soon turned to anger and Bahai Jaro wanted revenge against his miserly brother, so he put colourful clothes on his pet gibbon and released him near his brother's house. When Bahi Dampu saw the gibbon, he laughed, forgetting that Dayak people are forbidden to ridicule animals, that this is taboo. The gods, however, punished both brothers, sending down lightning and changing their two houses into stones.

There was so much money that this uncle owed us after years of collecting my mother's salary, that my mother thought we could manage to buy something in the town when we arrived there. And now my uncle disappointed my mother again. He didn't pay her back.

In Pangkalan Bun we moved several times from one rented house to another. My mother finally got some money from the bank — on credit — but my father never did anything about his brother, Ian. He didn't even get mad. He said, "Oh, he's my brother; if he dies, his children will live with us." Which is how it happened! Those children are very spoiled, too. They never go to work even though they live in our house. They do nothing, just sleep, eat in our house — for nothing.

Those two stones that were once the two brother's houses — the miserly brother and the bitter one — we can still see them in the village of Sekombulan and we believe that if we put a stick under one of them and make a wish, it will come true. Another thing about those stones is that from the middle of one of them we can climb up through a small hole and from the top we can see the peak of Mount Sabayan with the cloud that always covers it, the mountain where our people go when they die. Our deep heaven.

7

White Clothes

I<small>N SOME WAYS</small> life in the town was much different than in the village. In the village we can share everything we have without asking payment in return, but in the town you could not have the same unless you pay. In the village, neighbours care for each other, but in the town we found out that neighbours did not talk much to each other and most of the time compete about their belongings.

Most people in the village are Kaharingan or Christian but in the town where we lived most of our neighbours were Muslim and they do not like to be in touch with us because they think pork-eaters are dirty and can bring them sin. Even so, my mother was stone-hearted and said she would never go back.

When my father finally got a job in a rubber factory, he bought a push-bike. We were living in a rented house in an area called Kampung Raja (the village of the King).

Everyday my father rode his push-bike to Kampung Baru (new village), a couple of kilometres away. He had to supervise all the workers and make sure that they did the work right. The middle-aged Chinese couple who owned the factory were very mean, but not long after he started work there, they let us stay in one of the houses in the factory compound, so we packed all our belongings and moved to Kampung Baru, to yet another house.

The house was big and stood alone surrounded by the storage buildings where the workers kept all the rubber after pressing it flat and hanging it to dry before pressing it again into a tidy roll to send to Java. Father worked from early morning until the evening and his salary was small. My mother started off to school at 6 a.m. and came back in the midday, when she changed out of her uniform and went to the kitchen to cook lunch for all her children and husband. She brought foodstuffs from school because some women from Madura Island used to sell vegetables and fish carrying them in baskets on their heads. Mother could take the foodstuffs and pay them at the end of the month when she received her salary. She got roughly 250,000 rupiah a month and she had to send some money for my brother, who studied in the province, and pay our 5,000 rupiah school fee. Usually she had nothing left even for herself, but once in a while we could eat chicken or sometimes beef. She'd buy us clothes or other things on credit. She'd promise to pay at the end of the month, but by the beginning of the next month she had nothing left except a little money to buy us food. My father's salary only paid the rent.

I went to second grade, Lilis was in the first grade and Yayang was just two years old. She's very light-skinned and very pretty, but I feel different because I'm too dark. The old people in the village used to tell me to rub rice starch on my body to make it light.

Since we were poor, I used to play with anything around me. When the water got high I used to find some plastic toys collected on the banks and I always enjoyed them. The smallest things like dolls or plastic kitchen utensils I kept in a small box and I could spend hours playing with them. When we had the season for kite games, I didn't have any money to buy one so I would take some pieces of palm rib from the broom and make a kite from plastic or paper. It wouldn't fly high but I enjoyed the kite taking off for a few minutes before it fell back to the ground. When we had marble season sometimes I found marbles scattered on the ground. Then I would play games with friends and the loser would pay with a marble. I was good and when I won I could collect a lot!

Every month when my mother got her salary I was allowed to go with her to the market to buy rice, oil, salt, sugar and sometimes some cakes for the children. When I saw a toy, I wanted to have it. I'd sit there and beg my mother to buy it for me. At first she got very annoyed and tried to force me to move on, but mostly my tactic worked and my mother would buy me what I wanted. I remember one of the toys she got me at that market. It was a small plastic bag. I loved that cute bag and I used to keep some grain from flowers in it that I found on the way to school. My younger sister was very jealous of my little bag, but I hardly ever shared it with her.

I used to be jealous too if my mother bought clothes and gave the nicer ones to my sisters. I would think that she didn't love me as much as she loved them and I'd feel hurt. So my mother tried to buy the same style for all of us. Just the colours were different.

The house in the centre of the factory complex was big, with several rooms, and we lived there for almost ten years. But I will never go back, not after the experience I had there. Even now, sometimes at night I dream about somebody coming to my bed in that house to choke me.

It was a woman, I know that. Sometimes, in my dreams, I see her at the window — we had a window without curtains — and I see her passing with a horrible face and long hair. And this is really what happened there, but not only to me; it also happened to my sister. My father always said, "Oh, it's nothing, it's somebody walking past," but Lilis, every time she came home from school, passed the guest room and when she passed it, she ran, because she always heard somebody following her! Even in the first grade, in elementary school. When she asked my father why she heard someone but didn't see anybody, he said, "Oh, you're just feeling scared."

My elder sister Arita also dreamed in the night that a woman was trying to choke her. It happened many times, especially when she slept in the guest room. My brothers didn't want to sleep there because they always had bad dreams, but Arita slept in that room and every night she sat in the open window naked. My brothers saw her like that. And once she was cooking in our kitchen and Lilis came in and Arita said, "Don't ever come close to me again." Lilis was terrified. She told me Arita's voice was not her own, but I wanted to find out so I went in and she turned on me with a cooking spoon in her hand and screamed, "Don't ever come close to me!"

Nowadays, years later, she likes to go to church to pray; she does everything she can to be close to the church. She told us that she was aware of what was happening, but she couldn't refuse it. She said that when she was in that house, she always wanted to stay alone in the guest room. She said she didn't want anybody around her. She said every midnight she felt hot, really hot. She opened her clothes and opened the window and stood waiting. She said she always had a feeling that she wanted a man to come through the window. So almost the whole night she didn't sleep. She said she was standing there to save the family. She had a feeling he wanted to kill us. This went on many nights, over and over and over again. I know sometimes we heard things in that room, my sister talking to somebody.

My father decided she wasn't healthy in her mind. He thought that maybe she had studied too much, or was depressed. She went to the village doctor. He said nothing was wrong with her. But we had an uncle who was a paranormal. He could feel things before they happened. When we asked him to come, he slept in that room, and in the morning he said he really felt weary. He couldn't sleep the whole night. He had been hot and shaking and he had thrown the door of the bedroom open. He felt really bad. In the morning he made a cross in the window. He said it's not good to stay in a house with bad spirits. Later, when we moved away from that house, my father told us he had known something all the time. He didn't want to scare us but he said he, himself, saw the woman two times, the same woman in white with long hair. The face was beautiful, he said, and there was a smile, but it was more like a grin. He remembered that the pig in our cage had been really noisy. They have an instinct for that. Once my father saw her again in the evening. Behind the house there was a field; it was an empty field; nobody went there. It was surrounded by trees. And he saw the woman there, still the same, standing and grinning at him. He only saw her in the moonlight. We didn't have any electricity in that area. It was completely dark.

The owner of the house had told my father about the woman even before we moved in. He warned us. He's an old man. He'd been in the army before and he told my father "Just be careful of that house; if something happens. . . Just behave well, be careful." He said a woman had been killed in that house before. She was not a good woman. Somebody raped her and killed her. Then the owner sold the house. It was an old house. In the night, when I slept — in my own room — sometimes at midnight, when I was reading, I heard somebody knock, rapping on my door, and then knocking, three times, very loud. I felt terrible when I heard that, and in the morning I asked, "Who knocked on my door last night?" but my father always said, "Oh, just cats."

I knew that was impossible. My father had a cat, but it was always locked in the kitchen. In the morning, he was always still there.

We had lived in that house for many years and these strange things happened — not very often, not every night, but once in a while.

My father quit working for the rubber factory. He tried to get another job, but they said he was too old. They wanted younger workers. My father owned a small boat, and he went everywhere in the boat selling palm oil. I think he put all his money to buying lots of seeds. So he started another business. But he got so tired. The money was less and less.

When we moved, somebody wanted the house but my father told her not to live there. He told her what had happened to us, but she said she wasn't afraid. Just a couple of weeks later, she moved away. She said she didn't want to stay in the house any more. Yah! First she asked another girl to work there as a maid, but the girl said no, never. Then someone else moved in and stayed a couple of months. Now the house is empty.

My mother didn't know about these things because my father always protected her. He said my sister was out of her mind. And Mamah believed that. What Arita did was go to a praying group. They always prayed around her, and they would kneel and wash her. When they did this in Palangkaraya they felt that she was another person, not herself. Everybody in the group saw her change — she would be crawling around like a crocodile. The priest prayed and said a bad spirit had control over her and they must clean it.

Really, it's strange. After that she told us what happened. After she went to the cleansing, my sister asked us not to tell Mamah, because it was embarrassing. She said to keep it a secret.

The cleansing was her own idea. She didn't know what kind of cleansing she would have, but she watched from the sidelines for awhile, and when the priest asked her to come in the middle she said really she didn't think she would be able to talk and tell the priest what kind of feelings she had. But the people in that church were very good and they prayed over her. Somebody took a picture of her when she was crawling on the floor like a crocodile though, and she got mad and grabbed at the camera. She was already married by this time and had two children. When my sister went to the church, to this praying group, her husband wanted her to go to the medicine man. He said, "We should go there; they can manage with another power." But my sister was against that.

That house . . . even my brothers had bad dreams there, but they never felt like my sister. They tried to sleep together in that room, one in the bed and the other one down on the floor. One night, the one on the bed felt somebody choking him. He kicked my other brother because he thought he was choking him. When they realized that no one had been doing the choking, they said, "Oh no, we don't want to sleep here again." And from that time they slept in the hall in front of my bedroom on the floor.

Sometimes one or two workers would sleep in the small hut next to our house. They came from a country area and it was too late at night to go home. During the night, they always asked "Who's fighting?" They said they heard somebody fighting or crying at night at our house.

But what about the woman who was killed? Maybe she didn't want to die before the right time.

In town many things like this happen. My uncle heard that a woman came to an old Dutch house at night at certain times and he decided to find out for himself who she was. The house was empty. Nobody lived there at the time. My uncle began walking to and fro in front of it, and he saw a woman walking too, a beautiful woman with long hair, red slippers, long white clothes. It's strange, because it was the middle of the night. People say that long ago, everyone in the house was murdered. My uncle realized that something was wrong and decided to move as fast as he could!

The Dayak people had a big change of religion becoming Christian. We had missionaries come up many times, but still kept our own religion. On a Sunday we went to the church, and on the other days we gave offerings to the gods in the river, on the tree, on a big stone and in the grasses. Miniature things. We put eggs in small boxes, a piece of meat, rice wine, sticky rice. So the gods will not be angry. We have certain times to feed the gods. Our faith is very strong. Sometimes we just offer ourselves to the Christian religion, but our main faith is Kaharingan. The Christians have been up here only since before our Independence Day and mostly they don't ask people to change their religion. Mostly, Catholic missionaries from Germany came to us first, just to help. They gave food or medicine or other things. Then finally they gave a little bit of a sermon. You must be like this, help each other, something like that. They do some talking to all the people in the village. They say Christianity is growing bigger and stronger in this country, but it's very small compared to the Muslims.

With Muslims it's a little bit ugly the way they spread their religion. They have a paper around the town where they're spreading their ideas. They give the paper to Muslim boys and girls, but we get copies. We don't laugh at this way they spread their religion because they're dangerous. The paper says a boy must make love to a Christian girl, and then after she is pregnant he must ask if she wants to change religion. If she does, he will marry her. It's really an ugly paper. But this is one way to force us to change.

The Muslims always think that all Christians do is eat pork, so we are kind of dirty. After someone eats pork, they wash the knife or dish with soil, and wash it seven times so it's not dirty any more.

We had a young Muslim boy live in our house once. He came here from a small town and he got robbed where he slept. Somebody took his bag and he came to our house and stayed for a long time. He was doing nothing in our house, and every time I invited him to eat, he would always ask my brother, "What about that knife? Did you clean it with soil seven times?"

I heard that! He had something to eat in our house and talked like that. I was offended. When I asked him to move, I said, "We have too many people." I'd never done that before, but this Muslim boy was too much, because if he's going to be doing nothing, then it's better he move and try to find a job.

8

My Recipe Book

Now I know that my childhood was not really smooth. At first I got good attention from my parents, but after we moved from Kudangan village, their attention was getting lower and I felt left behind. I used to cross the river to the timber factory and collect waste wood which I cut into small pieces to make firewood. I cut them with an axe and carried them on my shoulder little by little. I had two older brothers, but they seldom helped as they said it would be embarrassing to look for wood — what if the girls saw them searching? They were grown-up boys and they did not want to embarrass themselves, so I took over the duty. My right arm was getting strong and muscled from cutting and carrying firewood.

My older sister Ita had her own duty of carrying water. We did not have a well, so we had to ask our neighbour a couple of houses away for clean water. Almost every afternoon she would carry the big buckets and take the water with a small dipper. She would fill the buckets and carry them back, meeting with a young handsome man who worked in the timber company across the river on the way home. My parents were upset to know that my sister tried to involve herself with a Muslim man. Papah warned her but my sister kept seeing him. They met each other secretly. My papah said this man came from south Kalimantan where they always want to marry non-Muslim girls and change them to be Muslim. Also he was only a labourer working in a factory. My parents wanted her to have a good, educated man. My sister was so depressed because she liked him. When she met him again, my papah came down to the river carrying his knife and wanted to kill the man. I was sad and nervous; I hadn't yet met Ahwa, but the story would be repeated with me.

My two brothers Uber and Eby, and my sister Ita, were studying in the Catholic junior high, a prestigious school because most of the high-ranking and best students in the town studied there. Ita got the highest ranking and was considered the cleverest student of the year. We even heard people saying she was the best one among all the students in Central Kalimantan province. My parents were so proud of that. Their effort to send all of their children to school was not wasted.

When I entered the same school, I finished as a runner-up. I didn't like the cooking lessons arranged by our headmaster's wife who worked there as a teacher. She was mainly teaching all the women's work: knitting, sewing and cooking and I always got a low score for all those subjects. When she was standing in front of the class writing recipes on the blackboard, I was busy writing at the back of my notebook, on the last pages — drawing and writing love stories. Often she thought that I was so serious with my writing that I was concentrating on her lesson. But sometimes Ibu Aryani — that's what we used to call her — would ask me a question abruptly and then she would know that I was not working on her lesson. She would complain about me in front of the other students. Anyway the back of my recipe book was full of my stories and during breaks some of my girlfriends would sneak back inside and read them when I was not around. I wrote about my feelings for one of the young police officers across the street from our school. I thought he was so handsome in his dark brown uniform. Often I'd sit in front of the Catholic church next to our school hoping to see him. I never knew his name but I named him in my imagination. Rondu, that was his name in my story. My friends were so anxious to find out who he was, but I never mentioned anything about him.

I saw Rondu many times wandering around in front of his post. My feeling was a longing for him but we never spoke any words and I knew that he never guessed that I had feelings for him or that I was sick with my longing. I was only a teenager of fourteen walking anxiously past the post full of young officers in my white and grey school uniform and a cloth bag strapped on my shoulder, my eyes searching secretly for Rondu.

❋

In an old Dayak story, a beautiful girl named Bawi Kuwu lived by the Kahayan River. When Bawi Kuwu had her first period, her parents put her in a stone cave. It was a tradition for the parents in Dayak Ngaju tribes to isolate their daughters and keep them from people's eyes until they married. Most girls from high-status families followed this rule. In isolation the girls prepared to be good wives. They learned how to weave and knit and cook (a little bit like Ibu Aryani's class!) and they were not allowed to go outside to meet people or to break the condition of isolation. Bawi Kuwu, kept for many years in the stone cave on the hill, was very beautiful. Her body was tall and slim and her hair like black silk grew to her heels. Her skin was soft and white as cotton. Her weaving was so gorgeous that many people came to her cave to barter for it in exchange for food.

The news of her beauty and weaving spread everywhere. Many people from different places came to meet her. Princes, rich men, poor men — they all came to see Bawi Kuwu, the girl who lived in the stone cave. They heard about her beauty and wanted her to be their wife. But when they came, they could not see her because she was inside the cave and many men were broken-hearted. They went home because Bawi Kuwu did not want any of them.

Mostly, when a girl was being isolated, the parents would choose a man from a good wealthy family to match up with their daughter. But none of the princes and handsome men from the far places was chosen for Bawi Kuwu. Those men were only able to see her hand to fulfill their longing, a hand that reached out from the inside of the cave for the food handed in to her, a hand so beautiful and white and soft.

One day a young man from another place across the sea came to see Bawi Kuwu. He was young and rich, but as happened with the other men, he also could not meet her. The man was so in love he could not handle his desire to meet Bawi Kuwu. He did not want to go back to his place without her. So one day he went quietly to her place of isolation with food he'd brought and waited. Not long after, a slim, beautiful hand reached out for the food through a small hole in the stone and the broken-hearted man caught the hand and held it tightly. Even as Bawi Kuwu struggled to pull her hand back, the man would not let it go. Because of the grief and pain in his heart at not being able to have Bawi Kuwu for his wife, he lost his mind and took out his knife. He cut off the beautiful hand and took it away with him and poor Bawi Kuwu bled to death in the cave of stone. Her life was over before someone was able to take her heart.

The story of Bawi Kuwu was one I sometimes heard when I was young, one of the stories in our tribe that go from mouth to mouth from one generation to another.

When I got my period, I was in elementary school in the fifth grade. I was twelve years old. But according to Mamah I was bigger than the other girls so that's why I got it earlier. One day I went home from school. I felt unwell. I couldn't describe the feeling but I went to pee many times that day and I couldn't sleep. When I went to the toilet just outside of the kitchen I saw dried black blood spotted on my underwear. I was terrified. I didn't know what it was. I hurriedly washed myself and my underwear and hoped that the blood wouldn't come back. I didn't dare to ask my mamah. I was so embarrassed. But the blood kept coming and when I ran out of dry underwear, I cut our old, thick blanket in very small pieces and put them on myself. For a few moments I felt better, then the cloth pieces got soaked again and I had to make new pieces and throw the old ones in the toilet.

Finally my mamah suspected something. She saw my underwear all over the washing line and found out the toilet was full of small pieces of cloth that had stuck there. She called me to the kitchen and asked me to explain and I felt the blood rush to my face. I wanted to cry, but my mamah cut small pieces of old towel, then folded them. I was uneasy with something else in my underwear but at least I felt better without having so much blood on them. I had to change every couple of hours so I soon ran out of these napkins again. But I found out that having a period is normal for women. Every woman has to have it. Before, I had no idea. For us, it was forbidden to talk about something like that. It was immoral. It was not common to talk about sex. It was taboo. It was terrible for the girl who didn't know anything.

One night I was trying to get to sleep. My sister was on the iron bed. I was down on the floor. That night, inside of my *kelambu* (mosquito net) I couldn't sleep. I felt uneasy. I felt something down under my stomach. When I touched it, I felt good. I kept touching myself and suddenly I found the hole and put my finger in it. I felt strange. I did not feel anything else but in a few moments I felt pain in my secret part as I moved my legs. I tried not to move all night. I tried to sleep. In the morning, I just forgot it right away. I didn't realize what I had done until years later when I married and had no first blood.

That ruined my marriage.

When I was fifteen we still lived in the old factory house and across the river was another factory. A man was working there taking care of the machines. I was with friends and we crossed the river. We had some kind of game, like volleyball, and he joined us. This was Ahwa. We didn't get close suddenly. It took months before we talked. Because I was shy. I was fifteen. He was old — thirty years old — but handsome! My parents didn't like him because he was Chinese. They tried to block our relationship. They don't like the Chinese; they say that they only think about money and don't like to be together with locals.

They asked my sister to follow me whenever I went down to the river for washing. She would come and join me, watching.

Even though he was on the other side of the river, Ahwa wasn't there to take a bath; he just came down to the river and hung up his towel! That's the way we recognized each other's presence. I would hang up my towel on my side; he would hang up his. We could see each other across the wide river, from a distance.

I think this happened for a couple of months, then — I had another way to meet him. We have a kind of lottery we call *porkas*, a kind of gambling that is all over the nation. Our government makes this lottery and Ahwa loved to play. He used to cross the river in the evening, and I'd wait in front of the house until he would pass by with his friends. No conversation, just looking at each other, because we knew it would be dangerous if my parents found out.

Finally we got a chance to talk to each other. One of my best friends had a Chinese boyfriend. So I went to her house because there, in that family, Ahwa and I could meet and talk.

My parents started to follow me when I went out. They said that I just wanted to meet with Ahwa. Ahwa couldn't stand it any more and said, "Okay, maybe after you finish with your school, when you are older . . . I'll stop my job here, for now. I'll go back home." His family lived in West Kalimantan. He gave me his address, but I lost it! I never saw him again. He was handsome and his eyes were slanting and sharp. He had delicate lips. I loved to watch him. When he moved away, I felt lost. I missed him, but he never came back, he just disappeared. My sister lost her first love and I did as well.

9

Customary Law

B Y THE TIME I WAS seventeen or eighteen I often went
out to meet my friends.

We lived near the centre of town and about four hundred metres away were two movie buildings. When evening
fell, I changed my clothes and got ready to go out. There were
many people, many of my friends and many people selling
food on the street. I really loved it there. My parents were
angry every time I went out. A good girl would not go out in
the night, so as not to embarrass the family name. But I kept
meeting my friends. And a boyfriend named Alexander. He
was not from Kalimantan but from Sulawesi. He was handsome with light skin. He said that his great-grandfather was
Dutch. We met on the street and then we went for a long
walk, talking about many things. We held hands and sometimes Alex kissed me. But one night we stopped and sat

down behind a building not far from our house. Suddenly Alex held me and kissed me all over and tried to flatten me on the ground. I was scared and fought him. He slapped my face and kept trying to do bad things to me. I kicked him and he released me and swore at me. I ran and left him there. I could not believe what he tried to do to me.

We never talked to each other again, but I got angry and jealous when I found out that Alexander had a relationship with one of my neighbours. He kept coming to her house and if I passed the place I could see them together.

I was very jealous and I hated them.

In the old house next door, my future husband Sam sometimes visited his friend and sat playing the guitar. He was living in his uncle's house, an ex-chief of Kinipan village by the Batangkawa River. His uncle was working as a member of the government legislature in the town and was a very respected man. I had just broken up with Alexander and we started to go out.

Sam decided to move to his friend's old wooden house next door. My parents didn't like it. Over there, they lived very simply. Sam studied in a different school. Every night he sat in front of his house playing the guitar. He was also handsome, tall with brown skin. But my parents said he came from a different tribe that had a lower caste than ours. Not only that, his father had married twice and the sons used to play around with girls. They used to be rich but now the boys were using all the antique jars to pay girls' families because the parents did not like them to play and sleep with their girls. They had to pay *kamuh*, customary law. In our villages, when a boy and girl are having something before they're married, they will get punished. The boy must pay maybe six empty jars to the girl's family, and promise not to do it again. It is called kamuh. He must pay for his mistake or leave the village for embarrassing the family name. And for my parents it would be embarrassing to have a son-in-law who came from this village, this tribe. My parents said he comes from the Batangkawa River, where the men are wild.

One day I told them I wanted to visit friends but I had promised to meet Sam, so I slipped away. I met him and we walked without knowing where. When the day was getting dark, we went to his aunty's ladang not too far from the river. I hadn't been there before. It had a small wooden hut in the middle of the ladang and he broke the lock and got in. When we arrived, the rain was pouring from the sky. And we were tired. There was a bed with a dirty, old mattress. We spent the night there kissing each other, holding each other but we did not make love. I was a virgin at the time. He asked me but I said no and went to sleep.

In the morning he woke up early and went to the garden and got some fresh cassava for our breakfast. We sat side by side and we were confused because we did not know where to go. I was scared of my parents but I had to go home.

When I got there, my father confronted me. He got a belt with a heavy buckle and beat me with it. My mamah did not want to talk to me and my papah hit me with the belt. It's iron or metal. It really hurt, but my feelings were more hurt. We were young, but nineteen is never too young for people here to know somebody. My father was beating me. I was growing up, and he was beating me in front of my brother and my sister and my mother. It was humiliating. I sat on a chair when he beat me and it hurt and I cried. I thought, he wants to kill me. I got bruised all over.

Afterward, I told Sam what happened.

He said, "Well, maybe you can run away." And I said, "Oh, no." I didn't dare to do it.

We went for a long walk to the town and came back at 10 p.m. and my family's house was already shut so we went back to his house. When he invited me to his room, I followed. There, we kissed each other and then, I don't know, it's a kind of stupid thing. We did not realize what was happening. It just happened. Something that we should not do. He just opened my underwear and entered me. I tried to push him away as it was very painful and he stopped. Then he found out that there was no blood, and that really ruined it. I never, never did anything like that before. But he didn't want to understand. He stood up and went to the chair and started questioning me. He said I did not have first blood. He said that meant I was having sex with someone else before him. I said that he was the first man but he did not want to believe me. He didn't want to understand.

In our culture it's very difficult. Men really want a wife to be a virgin so they cannot accept whatever reason we tell them. A virgin means blood on the first night. I didn't have it.

We kept seeing each other and every time we met, he still asked me the same question. He started to be rude, to fight me. I knew that if a girl did not have the sign of virginity, she would have trouble.

By that time I was attending my school tests to finish senior high school. It was considered to be the best government senior high school in my town and I passed the tests, but not Sam. He was not successful with his school and I heard that his family was very disappointed and thought I was the one who made Sam delay his success.

After that happened we had a distance between us. My family sent me away to Palangkaraya to continue my studies and stay with my sister. I had to have someone put eyes on me. I took a small plane, which was for only nine people including the pilot and the co-pilot, and I had to take a plane for the entire journey although if we have enough time we can take a cargo ship to Banjarmasin harbour. From there we can take the long boat with a single engine for a one day trip down to Palangkaraya. But, if the boat gets stuck in low tide, it sometimes has to stay overnight, until the high tide, before it can move again. My parents would not let me travel by ship and long boat as they did not think it was safe for a young woman to travel alone to an alien place.

My sister Arita picked me up at the airport and we took a taxi to the barracks. In a couple of days I would have to take the test to enter the university, but it was much the same as the senior high school test and my memory was still fresh so I had no difficulty.

After the test, I had to wait some weeks for the results. During those weeks I felt my head throbbing and I wanted to throw up all the time. I always felt cold. I did not know what was happening, but not long after that my oldest brother's wife came from the village up the river with her son and we soon became good friends. She asked me to check at the clinic so we went there and I felt my world fall as the nurse told me I was pregnant. A few days after, I told my sister. She was angry with me because she was not the first person I told. I said I felt ashamed and could not bring myself to tell her. She then sent a letter to my parents.

At that time my sister, Arita, was about to hold her wedding at my grandparents' and my mother told my sister not to let the family there know about my problem. She told her they would come to the wedding and take me back to Pangkalan Bun.

I tried to get rid of the baby. I jumped from the bed many times hoping the baby would fall. I ate young pineapple till my mouth almost burned, hoping the baby could not stand the food and would fall. But the baby was still there.

On the day my parents arrived, I was helping my sister make preparations, but all the time I felt weak and cold. My grandma put curious eyes on me and asked what the matter was. I pretended that nothing was wrong because if they knew, my family name would be spoiled right away and my sister's wedding might be spoiled too.

I was really scared because my family was very straight! And I also had the man angry because he didn't believe I was a virgin before. My mother . . . she really hated me. She said that I could not get married in our town as there are many people who know us and for sure they would ask why I was having to get married suddenly. To avoid people who were curious, we would have to marry in my husband's village on the Batangkawa River.

The village Sam came from is a small one, the same Kini-pan village that my family said was a place of disgrace. The journey would take three days by longboat, passing danger-ous rapids along the way. I had shamed all my family with this.

So we packed and my mamah presented me with a dozen glasses and a half dozen plates. I wrapped them carefully in a box. In the morning we departed from my town and started up the river. My husband-to-be, my father, Uncle Ether, his wife and their two boys, accompanied me. The boat owner, his wife and four-year-old son were also squeezed into the twelve-metre boat, which was full of bags and merchandise for the owner, a middle-aged man named Kilat, which means "lightning" in the Dayak language. He had a typically hand-some Dayak face chewing betel nut. He came from Nyalang village by the right Delang River to buy stuffs which he would sell in his village at two or three times the price. He bought sugar, salt, tobacco and seasoning. Also candy and cookies. The village where we wanted to go was on the left river and he would escort us there then go back to the right river and con-tinue his journey further on to his village, which takes two or three days.

The journey was long and tiring and we had to spend the night on the gravel on the riverbank because we could not reach the nearest village by late afternoon. So we went out on the gravel beach and bathed in the cold water. The jungle sur-rounded us and the night was falling quickly as we cooked rice and baked dried salty fish. I served rice for Sam and my papah and myself in an old plastic plate. I was sitting on the sand and eating my rice while the men chatted a couple of metres away. At the moment I was very sad. That night we slept on the boat, squeezing and curling our bodies to be comforted. It was so full that my papah and the owner Kilat slept on the beach. By midnight it was very cold and the dew was falling heavily on the earth. My blanket was wet and my body was shaking.

Early in the dawn while people still slept in the boat, the owner started the engine and took us up the river slowly. He had to be early as there was a risk of getting stuck in the low tide. We passed dense jungle and often he slowed the boat just to have a better view of some black monkeys we called *lutung*, now rarely seen as there are many Dayak hunters coming after their meat. Occasionally we saw pied hornbills, numerous macaques and proboscis monkeys. This longnosed monkey is a Dayak delicacy. If we do not get any pig or deer on our hunting trips, we go directly after the monkey. We cut the meat into thin slices and mix an amount of salt in it, then dry it in the sun. It can last for a couple of weeks if it doesn't get wet. Once my brother came back from hunting and left a longnosed carcass by the kitchen door. In the morning, when I opened the door, I was terrified by the carcass at my feet that lay with bulging eyes and a big fat stomach on the floor. I was so upset I could not eat anything that day.

There is nothing wrong with hunting monkey as long as we do not hunt them in the park. That's why Dayak people still hunt the rare monkey species such as maroon monkey, pig-tailed monkey and proboscis. Even the beautiful hornbill is hunted for its feathers although the hornbill is our holy bird and people arrive in heaven by its spirit.

On our journey, our boat passed many small villages. First when we departed from Pangkalan Bun town, there were only Malay villages dominated by Muslims. Further up were Dayak villages. I remember Kilat telling me a story of how we fought with the Dutch troops and eventually fled upriver, far away from towns. At the time, the Dayak were settled further down by Lamandau River in a place they called Kotawaringin Lama village. The Muslim people from other islands joined with the Dutch to fight the Dayak, who were bravely defending their own land. There was blood pouring on the earth but they did not give up. Then the Dutch got an idea about how to fight the Dayak and fired silver coins from a cannon right into the battlefield. The Dayak people were very excited by the coins and started to collect them and the Dutch troops fired real bullets at the Dayak warriors. Their bodies fell to the earth between the coins. The Dutch captured some of the warriors and sent them down the river, where they settled a village of their own named Pasir Panjang, which means long sand. Other Dayak warriors escaped by running up the river and settled their village where the troops would not come after them. So most of our people live inland. The villages are mostly far away from towns. And they live as farmers and jungle collectors. They harvest jungle material.

Sam and I were going to be married in his village. My mother didn't want to come, just my father. We went to the church, we went to the government, we got all the official letters. When we arrived we spent a few days in his brother's house. At his parents' house they prepared food, killed pigs and chickens and made decorations for the wedding, which was held in a longhouse, the biggest and longest one in the village, which could hold hundreds of people. The wedding was being held hurriedly but we prepared a lot of food because when there is any party the villagers from up and down the river will attend. They don't need an invitation as they think a party is for all the people. We killed many pigs and chickens and many people came and brought chickens as a contribution. Others brought rice or sugar or coffee powder to help with the wedding cost. My pregnancy was a couple of months already and I was always sick in the morning and throwing up. My health was very bad so I could not really help.

The longhouse was decorated with palm leaves. We use palm a lot for our life here. We use the rib to make a broom and often when we have a party we select a tree and cut it to get the shoots for vegetables. We can get a lot of shoots from one tree. We cut it into small pieces and mix it with pork or chicken meat. The trunk we leave in the ladang and after a couple of weeks we can cut it again and harvest the fat tree larvae. A kind of insect lays its eggs in the rotten palm trunk and the fat white larvae is a delicacy. Once I remember my brother looking for larvae while waiting for our papah. Because the worms were crawling everywhere, he decided to keep them in my pocket and I could feel them moving. We used to fry them without oil as they contain high, rich fat. They're tasty and sweet. I like to watch when my brother fries them alive. He pours them in the hot frying pan and the worms are moving and jumping. Soon they're fried in their own fat. My mamah cannot stand to see these little round creatures moving and fried to death in her frying pan.

Back to the wedding preparations. The wedding long-house was only one plain long room and at the rear it was connected to a kitchen. We build them in that style for the reason that we hold many parties and need the space to hold hundreds of people. If we want to sleep, we just spread a grass mat on the floor. For a husband and wife there is no privacy in such a house. They can be together if everyone else is asleep. The other choice is that they can be in the ladang away from people.

Many people had already come and were staying in the village waiting for the day. Many were old friends of my parents who heard we were being married and came from up the river just to attend the party. We prepared jars of rice wine as well. Dayak people like to drink and get drunk so rice wine (or *tuak*) would be the most important thing during the party. A few weeks before we arrived, my husband's family was already making it from brown rice. They cook the brown rice and let it cool on a plain bamboo mat. After that they mix in the ragi (fermented flour) and put the rice in jars and seal it. In a couple of days there will be juice and it can stay for months or even years. Most rice wine is made from brown rice. We do not make palm wine as other Dayak do, such as Dayak Iban.

Our wedding party was held very quickly — only two days. Usually it would take more. When the day came, my aunty put the white wedding gown on me. The dress was very pretty and long. I stayed in Sam's brother's house and he stayed in his other brother's house as there is a taboo to be together on the wedding day before being blessed by the priest. So when I finished getting dressed, I went down to the village walking by the small stony village road. Two young girls were holding my wedding dress behind and I had to walk slowly as the shoes I used were with high heels. The sharp heels sometimes stuck in the clay earth so I had to be extra careful. My papah, my uncle and my aunty accompanied me.

Close to the church, the groom was waiting by the road. There were many people waiting there. Sam wore a black suit with dark blue pantaloons. He looked very handsome in his suit. The people were trying to get a closer look at me. My wedding dress apparently attracted them. The crowd was moving slowly to the nearby church. We went in and the priest was waiting. We sat right in front where they put four chairs in a row. I sat on the right, Sam was on the left and the two young girls were by both sides. The priest asked us to stand up. He said our promise to be husband and wife. I did not know what I felt at that time. I felt plain. I did not feel either happy or sad. The ceremony just flowed like it had to. After it finished, we went down to the longhouse where the party was; there were many people already there. The Dayak music was pounding hard as we entered and sat in the middle of the room on two chairs. In the corner was the gamelan group and surrounding us were the people. Every eye tried to get a better look at us. In a few moments the food was served in long rows on the floor. People started to eat after praying. We do not use spoons. We wash our fingers and eat with them. Everybody tried to eat as much as they could. Meat is expensive and only at a party can we enjoy a lot of it.

After everybody finished eating and the dishes were taken back, the music was pounding again and people started to dance — four at a time. They dance by turn. Mostly the old people or the people with high status are granted the first dance. First they would greet each other by moving a hand towards them. Man to man, woman to woman. They toast and drink the rice wine, then start to dance.

There are numerous co-dancers trying to feed them rice wine all the time and they have to drink it. They pound their feet on the floor and scream happily. Everybody enjoys it and most of the people there except children have their turn to dance. By afternoon the party was finished and we went back to the house. Now I stayed with my husband in his parents' house. A lot of people still stayed in the longhouse or the village.

Late in the afternoon, my husband's family brought my clothes as I no longer stayed at his brother's. I felt very tired. My papah came in. Somebody escorted him as he was really drunk. He'd been arguing with my husband's uncle who was also drunk. My papah said that this uncle was a black magic follower and could take his head off his body and fly, looking for people's blood to suck. The uncle started to be angry with him. Everybody in the house tried to calm both of them. My papah repeatedly said that the uncle would never manage to harm him with his black magic. The uncle retreated to a corner and my papah finally fell asleep on the floor. We then retreated to the room provided by his parents. It was small and there were two kapok mattresses spread out on the floor. That was our wedding bedroom. It used to be his sister's room before we came. His parents' longhouse was a bit different from the normal longhouse in the village. They had two bedrooms. One for us now and the other one for Sam's stepmother's son and his wife who spent most of their time on the ladang. Every couple of weeks they would be back to see the four-year-old daughter they had left with his mother. The little girl was pretty like her mother, light-skinned and very clever, but she was very shy with me. She hardly missed her parents as she spent most of her time with her grandparents.

One evening her parents came in from the ladang. They paddled their canoe against the stream and brought home a big bamboo cylinder. It contained pieces of snake meat. The husband told us excitedly the story of how they killed the snake which was as long as one and a half metres and big. So that night everybody had a dinner of snake meat. We sat together around the kitchen floor and they passed the bamboo cylinder by turn. Everybody took a big piece of the meat which was steamed with salt in the bamboo. My husband took one and said to me that I better not eat it because I was pregnant. But I felt everything in my stomach wanted to get out. I hardly ate my rice. Even though the kerosene lamp we used was not too bright, I still remember the meat was white and fishy and the batik motif skin was still left on some of it. I did not touch it at all. We finished our dinner, the family kept on chatting, and as the time crawled to midnight we went to our room.

10

Built From a
Young, Live Tree

AFTER THE WEDDING DAY passed, many people went back to their villages or back to their ladangs. We arranged a trip to the village where I was born, going by long boat, and the journey took some days, passing the dangerous rapids. We came up to the other river, to the head of the Delang to stay in my uncle's house. This uncle is named Dehes and he is my father's youngest brother — the only one of those children left in Kudangan. The family has a big rubber ladang and my father had asked Sam to work there and make money for when I would be giving birth. We lived in my uncle's house which was very small and had only one bedroom where my uncle sleeps with his wife and three of his children, but we got a place to sleep in an open back room.

In the day time they used the room where we slept for other things, so early in the morning we had to wake up and fold the grass mat we used and place it in the corner. My husband went to the ladang and tapped rubber but he was still young and liked crowds; the jungle did not make him happy. He tapped the rubber carelessly and often tapped the young trees so the sap hardly came out. If he was late to go in the morning the sap was sometimes dry, since it is only possible to get a lot of sap in the dawn when the air is still cool and fresh and the sun has not yet come up.

A few days after we arrived in the village, my Uncle Ian in Sekombulan — the one who later got murdered — invited us to visit. He said they were going to make a *babuhung* party for the people in that village because they had opened a new ladang and people had helped with cutting, burning and planting. So they had to make a party to thank the ones who had helped them and there would be lots of food and rice wine. They would slaughter pigs and chickens to feed people. They would dance all night with *bagondang* music. So we walked up in the morning by the small river path, passing old ladangs, small streams and sometimes new ladangs just ready to be planted. I got leeches on my legs which I just pinched off. Blood streamed down as the bites were open. My father and my rich uncle Ether were also with us and my uncle's wife. On the way, Sam almost stepped on a ground centipede. He took a piece of wood and intended to kill it right away but my papah rushed to him and firmly asked him not to kill it. "It's taboo to kill any kind of animal when your wife is pregnant," he said. "The animal you kill could put a curse on your baby," he explained.

After a long walk, we arrived in the afternoon in Sekombulan, the last village on the border of West Kalimantan, standing in a valley surrounded by hills. The peak of Mount Sabayan, our deep heaven, stood in the distance covered with cloud. The village was small and tidy. We greeted people who were coming in from their ladangs, carrying their ladung, the rattan basket. When we got to my uncle's longhouse, they invited us to come in. My aunty was pretty and nimble so no wonder my Uncle Ian fought with my grandparents to marry her. My grandparents did not agree that he marry her because they said she liked to hang around with men before she met my uncle. They did not like the girl but my uncle insisted. She was known as the *bunga* Sekombulan, the flower of Sekombulan.

So we sat together on the floor which was covered with rattan mats and drank coffee together. In the morning my aunty and I helped the women cooking in the kitchen to prepare for the party that night. Some men were collecting firewood and wild spices from the forest nearby or slaughtering pigs and chickens, but many were helping in the ladang planting the seed. The men would stand in rows and make small holes with a stick and behind them the women were bowing their bodies, filling the holes with seed and covering it right away with soil to prevent birds eating them. The meals were provided by the owner of the ladang. That night they would have the babuhung party with music and rice wine. There would be a lot of food — chicken, pork — and people could have as much as they wanted.

The babuhung held in Uncle Ian's house was quite big. In the evening the people from all over the village gathered there — young, old — no matter whether they had helped in the ladang or not, they joined the party. My uncle was fortunate to have enough money to hold this because he also had another business as a merchandizer. He bought stuffs to sell in Sekombulan from Tumbang Titi town in West Kalimantan. The stuffs were in rows at the front of the house.

All night the bagondang was pounding hard while people ate. Soon after they finished eating, the women collected the dishes and cleaned up the room for dancing. Two men and two women went to the dance floor. They were given long cloths by the man who was leading. They got up, wrapping the cloths around their waists and started to greet each other with their hands together. After that they kneeled in the middle of the room and toasted and drank the rice wine before they stood up to dance. The dance was slow and soft like a hornbill's movement and they followed the rhythms of the bagondang music. Everybody looked happy, dancing and getting drunk. The party finished at dawn.

Some men too drunk to get up slept on the floor.

In the morning we packed up and left the longhouse and went back to Kudangan. Each of us carried a live suckling pig in a woven bamboo cage. My uncle gave us these pigs to thank us for helping and joining the party. We walked along the timber road which winds thousands of kilometres all the way down. The timber company had made that road about five years before to transport their logs from the forest. It was a long and hard walk, up and down hills carrying my noisy pig who was always humming, moving and screaming. My legs were swollen when we arrived in the afternoon.

Everybody was exhausted. The next day my papah, my uncle Ether and his wife packed up and left the village by longboat. They were going back to Pangkalan Bun. My husband and I were staying.

It was hard. I had hard times with my husband because I was older than he by a few months and he always said that I was too old for him. He seldom went out with me because he did not like to be with an old lady. It's really not common for us to marry with the woman older than the man and soon there is always talking around. People look at you strangely. We had that problem many times when we were in Kudangan. When we were there Sam sometimes disappeared for the whole day and one of my cousins told me that he joined a girl in her parent's ladang. I tried not to believe that. My stomach was big already and one night I asked him about it. "I would never have a girl friend whose earlobes are not normal," he told me. The girl had a bit of problem with her earlobes being too small. But Sam kept seeing her and my cousin sometimes reported this to me. She had seen him again. The girl was her classmate in junior high school and they were good friends.

Once we went to the ladang and one of the neighbouring farmers noticed that the stilts of our hut were built from a young, live tree. He came to my husband and asked him to cut the tree as it is forbidden for a pregnant wife to be in a hut whose stilts are made of a live tree. I would have difficulty when I wanted to give birth. So my husband cut the tree. When I left the town, my mamah had given me some pieces of root and she said I had to consume them everyday. The root would prevent the baby from contracting something during the pregnancy. For instance, if I do not like some-body's face or behaviour, there is a possibility the baby would be similar. Also she said that every day I should try to get jasmine flowers and keep them near me. I asked why and she said that jasmine would bring the baby beauty. So when I was in the village I always searched for the flower.

Sam and I got only a little rubber and very little money. My father had given this work to Sam but he didn't do it. He just did what he liked and there was no money — we were broke. The rubber trees were abandoned. I was sad and worried because my stomach was getting bigger and soon we would have a baby and needed money to pay the expenses. My husband did not really care. Once I found that the little money I had collected was gone. He took it to buy rice wine with his friend. I was angry and tearfully asked for the money from him, but he said he had worked hard for that money and deserved to spend it anyway he liked. I couldn't say anything more because he would never listen to me. He hit me, he forced me many times, many times. I had no chance. I thought of my family . . . that . . . they didn't expect me back. So I didn't have a place to run. My uncle also wanted to get rid of me because he didn't like my husband. My husband was so handsome, but lazy, I can say that!

The old teacher named Omas Kroma still lived in our village. Once he was a respected man and many people came to him and sought his advice, but time went by and soon our government began to send young people from the town to take every position in the village. Young people preferred to go to their own teachers for advice. So when Omas Kroma retired he was forgotten. People thought he was crazy because he sometimes spoke Dutch. Old people, our people, remained in their old-fashioned positions in the village and maintained their old tradition of hunting and farming and old Omas Kroma was desperately still speaking his Dutch that once had made him special. His wife, Indai Ungking, was a midwife, my youngest sister born in her hand. She treated my mamah's pregnancy and when I came back to the village she treated mine as well. When I was there she used to come twice a week, rubbing my stomach. She came with coconut oil in a small coconut shell which she mixed with crushed onion, and she grabbed and scratched my stomach, me, lying on the grass mat on the floor, my husband waiting close by the door.

Mamah had given birth every two years until there were seven of us. There was no contraception ever mentioned. She stopped when we moved to the town, where she used local medicine she took from a kind of creeping plant behind our house. She collected the small berries and swallowed them with her coffee. I was in elementary school and I asked her what the berries were for and she refused to answer as there would never be any discussion about those things — not even when I was grown up. When I went back up to the village with my Dayak husband, most young people who married had better treatment and they followed our government program called *keluarga berencana* of having only two children, even though a few wanted to have more. There was a local clinic for the public and a permanent nurse and a temporary doctor working on duty. The conditions had improved since my mamah's time, but when I was there, I seldom went to the nurse because it was very expensive and sometimes we had to be sure that they were not away in their ladangs.

My husband tried to open a wet rice field. For more than a week he cultivated the wet ground where my grandfather had grown brown rice, and soon the rice was freshened by the water and grew green and rich. I was happy to see it from our small hut that my husband had built from pieces of wood and thatch. In the morning I followed him to the ladang which we reached by canoe and by walking past my uncle's rice field. There we spent most of our day. Before work my husband would go to the old ladang, make a small fire and bake some cassava. The smoke also kept mosquitoes away. For lunch we brought rice from home and he would catch small fish from a little lake called Lake Potung with a woven basket. At the time my blood pressure was very low and I was always hungry with the baby needing to feed too. Sam was not able to bring me to the public health centre to get an injection of medicines. We did not have money. We could not even give money to my uncle for helping us.

After a couple of months Uncle Dehes changed. He hardly spoke to us any more and he talked about us to other people. That made me ashamed but I could not say anything while my husband spent any money we got from selling rubber for more rice wine and he also made a relationship with the young girl in our village. People were talking behind us and I could not go out to meet anyone. Sam made his family, who owed him some money, pay him and he began cutting rattan. He paid some boys to work for him and behaved as if he was a big boss. The boys were working for him cutting the rattan but most of the rattan was too young. Sam waited at home playing his guitar while the boys were working to get as much rattan as they could without thinking about the quality. Every week Sam paid them and collected the rattan. When the money was almost gone, he made a bamboo raft and loaded the rattan onto it. Again he had to pay a villager to help him raft down the river to deliver the rattan to his family. He was away for two days and came back with little money. This made his spirit even lower. Once I saw him take my uncle's rubber and mix it with his and sell it at a shop in the village. I didn't dare to say anything as he was a hot-blooded man. He could put his hand on me even though I was in a big pregnancy.

One day I went with my cousin to our ladang and he came with us and I said something that didn't please him. I said *jaman*, which means age, like time, but his father's name is Jaman, and for Dayaks it's forbidden to say the father's name. Very forbidden. Especially in a Dayak village. It's a rule there. For my father-in-law I should show respect.

I forgot that I had to use another similar word instead of that one and suddenly Sam pulled out his knife and almost stabbed me. He was holding me down, fighting me. I was very scared.

Then he became calm and we walked to the ladang. I was holding the basket for seed. I was eight months pregnant. I said to my cousin, "Stay close to me." She was about eleven years old. So when we got to the ladang, I walked behind Sam but he laughed softly and without warning turned around and slapped me in the head. I tried to keep my balance and before I understood what had happened, he took his knife again and almost stuck me in the stomach. My eyes were dark and I blindly snapped him with the bamboo basket I was holding. Luckily, he did not fight back. He left me there, alone. My cousin ran back to the village. She was so frightened that she ran and crossed the river by swimming rather than waiting for my husband to paddle her by canoe. It was dangerous, since there is sudden flooding which often comes down from the head of the river.

My husband left me alone but I was so frightened and angry that I didn't care that I was alone in the jungle. When the sun slowly went down and the evening fog came, I tried to go to my uncle's ladang and sit in the hut. The surroundings were quiet and the night insects were coming out and making their noise. Then my husband came and asked me to go home. I didn't want to go with him but it was not safe to be outside where sometimes a huge wild boar or snake or even bears come out.

Later on, I found out that my aunty was very anxious to hear her girl's report and forced my husband to pick me up from the ladang. She was upset because I was in big pregnancy and it's taboo to be outside in the jungle in the late afternoon as we believe that evening is a time for bad spirits and evil to come out. Children should be inside to avoid the bad spirits and it is forbidden for a woman who is pregnant to be outside since the baby is fragile and might be disturbed by such evil.

11

Forty Days

WHEN I WAS SMALL my uncle's neighbours had a couple of jambu trees behind their house so I used to climb the trees and take as many fruits as I could. The neighbours were nice to us. Now after many years I'd come back to see if some of the childhood memories were still there. These neighbours were getting old. The husband was suffering from TB and they did not have money for medicine. Their boy was married to a thirteen-year-old girl who could not even take care of herself, so the husband always looked after her all the time. She was beautiful and the husband said that she was like a piece of ginger, the more you chew it, the more heat you feel on your tongue.

Sam never managed to get any money and he always went around with girls. When I heard that my parents said if I wanted to come home, they'd accept me, I decided to go. Sam agreed to by river with Uncle Ian from Sekombulan, who, with some other men, was sending forty-five pigs to Pangkalan Bun. While they journeyed by river, I walked many kilometres with my aunty and her niece all the way from Kudangan to Nyalang village. I walked with my bag and my almost-ready-to-born child. At Nyalang my aunty got a boat. She invited me to ride with her until we met with the men and the rafts where the river divided. Sam and I continued along the Batangkawa River to Kinipan village because Sam wanted to visit his family. The others continued down the Lamaundau River to Pangkalan Bun, where they all stayed with my parents.

Sam and I went to his village. His family wanted me to work, although I had low blood pressure and was so weak. When they pounded the rice in the rice mortar, they said I must help them.

Once, when I helped, my husband came and got another long iron stick to pound with. We began to laugh because I was so glad that he finally joined me. When we pound, it has a rhythm, but my stick touched his and he got angry. I was barely able to move at the time; my stomach was heavy and my feet were swollen. He could not accept that I moved too slowly with my pounder in the mortar and so he started to fight me. He treated me like an animal because he said I tricked him, that I'd been wild with other men before, and he didn't find me a virgin.

My husband has a step-mother because his real mother died of TB. Sometimes, when we ate together with his family, it seemed that I was always hungry with the baby. If I took a little bit more, they would seem to say, "Ugh! You are getting greedy!" I was shy to ask for more rice. Sometimes, when they didn't stay home, I went to the kitchen and prayed to find something to eat but they hid the food away so I didn't have a thing.

After many days we got a boat and continued to Pangkalan Bun. We went straight to my house. My mother, my father, they were good. My mother was still a little bit distant with me, but she accepted me in their house. Sam gave me to my family and then he went back to his village. My father and my mother never let me work, not even to lift the water for bathing. They even washed my clothes. . . . It was very different. And I always got the bed. They knew that I had low blood pressure. They asked me many times to go to the doctor to be checked.

Then I got better. I even got high blood pressure! The nurse said it was too high, very dangerous, because I could get bleeding when I gave birth. When my time came, I wanted to give birth at home but my nurse said it was too dangerous and they sent me to hospital. I went with my mamah and papah and they put me in a room not for having a baby but for examinations. Just a short table with foot stirrups. In the other room was a woman who was crying and shouting, giving birth. When I heard her I felt really scared. I think there were two nurses. My father came in, lots of visitors — they came in to have a look! I said, "Oh, no!" I was very angry. But they kept watching.

Finally I asked the nurse to get rid of them, and she closed the curtain. The other woman kept screaming and screaming; it was terrible, and my spirit was low and I got to trembling. And when my time came, the baby almost fell on to the floor! There was nothing under me to hold her, no table under us.

At first I didn't want to see her. I didn't know if the baby was perfect or not; maybe no leg, no arm! I closed my eyes. When I opened them, I saw the baby was yellow, very yellow and some stuff — I don't know what kind of stuff but it was yellow — covered her everywhere.

The baby looked dirty. They said it was because when I was pregnant I liked to eat palm sugar, all the time, day and night. They said that's why the baby did not look clean but had some yellow stuff all over her body. They moved me into a different room, and put the baby in another room with the other baby. Just two of them, in a room by themselves. I stayed in my room with some women — not just after they gave birth, but women with different sicknesses. It was so hot and we couldn't open the window, because they prohibit it. It was hot and dirty. The whole first night the baby was crying. And the other baby just kept quiet. The nurse was not always there. She was always on the hospital phone. She never looked at the babies or at us. Finally my mamah put some cotton in water and gave it to the baby's mouth. She liked it.

In the morning they brought the baby to me to nurse. At first it was really hard. It was sore. They said because the baby's tongue was sharp. I tried, but my left breast was so swollen. Sometime in the morning the doctors came and checked us. The food was really bad, just dry rice. But the baby must have had enough milk. We put her back to sleep, but again in the night, she was crying and crying. One woman who was in a bed by the door said, "Oh, look, it's a black dog, he just crossed to the other room." Everybody was scared! Why did the nurse let this black dog come in?

The nurse arrived, and my mamah asked her about it. She said, "We never let dogs come in."

They searched around — no black dog.

We were sure the dog was not a real one. Many women died from birthing there, and we believed their spirits were restless and that they wandered around where they died, showing themselves in the forms of animals. The dog could be a ghost. That's what most patients in the room believed and also me and my mother. These spirits can disturb and steal a child's soul.

I said to my mamah, "Try to get the baby to me. Don't wait for that woman any more" — because the nurse didn't allow us to have our babies. It wasn't safe. There were too many sick people. My mamah went out and got my baby. She put her on my stomach. The baby! I didn't give milk, but she went to sleep.

Ah! But what about the black dog! My mamah was afraid of it and said, "We can't keep the baby here. I don't want to go to that room any more!"

I took the baby home after three days. I had no health insurance and could not afford to stay any longer. About forty days after that my husband finally came to the house to look at her, and he said, "See its eyes are just like mine. But only her eyes!" He said the baby wasn't his, that it could be maybe a neighbour's kid or something like that. He wanted to force me to do . . . with him. Forty days is not really healthy for a woman to, and he forced me to do something of husband and wife. Then he stayed with us for some weeks and I tried to refuse all the time because it's not good for a woman having sex after giving birth. I was never the same to him any more, because I thought he might hurt my baby. He got angry and said I'm a prostitute, that the baby was not his. My parents were eating in the kitchen, and he came in with a knife and grabbed my hair and said he was going to kill me. My father rushed in from the kitchen and took the knife and Sam ran away.

After three days, he came back, telling me he'd met Alex, my old boyfriend. When Sam joined an exhibition for boxing, Alex was part of it. They held the exhibition in the town, in the football field. Many people came to watch. The games would also show off the best boxers from West Kalimantan.

But before they started, Sam met Alex and Alex teased Sam and said Sam only got what was left. Sam cancelled his part in the games and wandered around trying to find Alex, who had disappeared. He believed what Alex had said, even when Alex told him that he'd been sleeping with me when Sam was away and I was still pregnant! I said that Alex was trying to destroy our marriage, but Sam did not want to listen. That night he found out that Alex was visiting his new girlfriend, my neighbour. He chased him and almost stabbed him and Alex ran to the military compound half a kilometre from our house. He had an uncle who worked there.

The next morning some police came for Sam and took him to the police station. He was put in jail. They put him in a small room just like a cage next to the guard room and tortured him. The next morning I went to the police station and they asked me some questions. I told them that Alex had come up with his lies and the police looked surprised but the next day they tortured Sam more. My father gave the police some money and even gave one of them an antique jar, but still Sam had to stay in that cage for almost two months before they sent him to the main jail outside of town.

I tried to be patient. When he was still in the cage I used to visit him. I took our baby when he asked and brought him food and cigarettes. One morning my father escorted me with the baby to the cage. He stayed outside and I went in with a police guard and sat next to Sam with the baby on my lap. In front of us was a fifteen-year-old boy who was eating his rice package. "He stole clothes from the prostitutes' complex," the policeman said to me, and suddenly kicked the boy's back with his boot when he noticed him trying to wrap and save his little rice. The rice spilled. "Clean it up!" the policeman ordered him.

My eyes caught a pile of rags in the corner full of blood and I saw a young man sitting there in the dark, his lips swollen and his eyes cloudy. There was dried blood on his face. My husband's face was not in good shape either, and he said the day before, at noon, "They pulled my nails with pincers because I kept asking to go to the toilet."

The day before, at the same time, our baby had been sleeping in the rocking swing and suddenly she woke up screeching. Her face turned red. We were panicked and I grabbed and held her, trying to comfort her. She was moving and crying like she was in real pain. Then a few minutes later she was easy and stopped crying. I tried to find if something had bitten her, but there was nothing.

They tortured her father at the same time as her painful crying.

Sam spent half a month in the main jail before he was released. The accusation was of carrying a knife which they said was "against the law." Nothing was mentioned about Alex.

Sam went back to his village not long after he was released. Although he said his work would require him to stay in the jungle a few months, he didn't come back for almost a year and then only to visit once. Later, I heard that he had another girl about fifteen years old. They were together for months and he spent his money to buy her clothes and new sandals, so we never got any money from him.

When I heard about the girlfriend, I went up to his village and stayed several days. Sam was living with his boss, doing woodcutting. He paid some money to live there.

When I found out that the story about the girl was true, I asked him to take me to the girl's house. He didn't want to, but I insisted. We went to see the girl, and I met her parents. My husband went into the girl's bedroom. She was lying down. He asked her to come out and meet me. They were just like husband and wife!

I didn't get angry at all with the girl. I said, "You're still young, why would you do something like this, with another woman's husband? If you wanted him, you can ask him to marry you, not just play." And the girl cried.

I told her parents that if their daughter wanted my husband, I would ask only for a divorce letter, and then they could be married. Her mother was crying, and the girl was crying also.

When we left to go back to the boss's house, my husband almost stopped me with the knife again. One of his boss's daughters saw him and screamed. My husband's boss took his side. But not his wife. She arranged a kamuh ceremony for me because if we have something like this, if a husband is going wild with another girl, then we can ask him to pay us. A kind of punishment. His boss's wife paid with eggs and rice, and my husband tried to be nice. Before the ceremony started, he said, "Why do something like this? I realize that I'm wrong, I want to go back to you, back to our child."

The girl was there too, and they paid a little bit of money to me — I think about 45,000 rupiah as a substitute for three antique jars they didn't have — and promised that they wouldn't do it again. The girl's family paid me that for what she had done with my husband.

Everything was better for one or two days. But then I saw that girl insulting me, laughing about me, in a bad way. I asked Sam to escort me back to Pangkalan Bun and he did. He spent one night there and in the morning he moved back to the village.

After that, I wrote to him asking for a divorce letter, and asking him to marry the girl. I was willing to give him to her. Somebody told me when he got the letter, he was crying and couldn't believe what had happened. He was thinking that I would accept everything, be nice. He wouldn't even divorce me.

I waited and waited, but no answer. Everything was over. It's something I want to forget about.

Once, much later, when my baby was about three years old, Sam came back. He brought maybe two million rupiah. He just wanted to come to my home and ask, "Can I spend the night here?" And I said, "No!"

"Okay, maybe you want to go rest for awhile," he said. When I went to my room, he counted the money in front of his daughter. He said to her, "Don't call me 'uncle'." She had called her father uncle because all men are uncle for everybody. And he said, "No, call me Papah."

I heard this from my room and I called my daughter to come into the room, and I said, "Don't *ever* say that — Papah."

My daughter began to cry.

He counted out lots of money but never gave us any, not even one thousand rupiah. And I felt, Ach! What a man!

I told him, "Don't ever say that this baby is yours! You have no claim on her." I burned all the letters we had and some of our photos, wedding pictures. I made a letter, but it's just to the chief of his tribe. Since I don't have the wedding letters any more, I couldn't go to the government and ask for a divorce. I don't want to look for our records, I guess because I don't want to put his name on my baby's papers or on her birth certificate. So she doesn't have one. Because I don't want to put his name on it, ever.

I was nineteen when I married and I've been alone ever since.

12

Work among
the Men

KARINA. IT'S KIND OF a Western name. I say, Karina
Hagafiona Monica. Karina means "pure." I found this
name in the Greek language. Then Hagafiona is from the
Dayak language. It means "to take hope." And Monica is
something I don't know. It's just nice!

For now life is easy for Karina, because she started elementary school where my mother's teaching, and they don't
ask for a birth certificate. I thank my family, because they
took her in. My baby, she's very adorable to them. She's
clever and loves to play chess. I think she's the granddaughter that they love most. I think because she was born near
them. My father has about five or six grandchildren — but
the others are far away. Just my child always stays with them.

Sometimes they say if I want to go somewhere with my child, I can't. I think I will never be able to take her with me. They love her very much. They say if I marry and my husband will accept her, then they would give her up to us. If not, she will stay with them for ever. So I stay too.

I tried to get some money for myself. Because my mother had a small canteen in her school, I bought children's snacks and I was selling them in the canteen — only a little profit — two or three thousand a day. I was saving it and I managed to take a course, a typing course for three months, then an English course for six months, then computer for three months.

I went to school for two or three hours every night, but the whole day I would spend with my baby. If I had to be away longer than two or three hours at night, I had equipment to suck all the milk out. All this time I had no extra money, and no job.

In 1993, my tutor, Mr. Thomas, who was teaching me English, asked me to help him with his "guests." He worked for Kalpataru Tours, and when they had a big group, they needed assistants. He was from Flores and a well-educated man.

I also knew a manager with Kalpataru Tours — his name was Monti — who encouraged me to become a guide. "Think of it. If you become a guide, you would be a pioneer, the first woman guide in Kalimantan," he said.

My English was not good yet and I was afraid when I talked I would make mistakes. Sitting in front of blond tourists and tumbling over broken words was a nightmare. My knees were trembling and my mind was somewhere else, but the manager's encouragement helped me and after that,

I helped him and Thomas a lot. When I went to Tanjung Puting National Park with them, I never got paid and even after I had already helped many times, I was still broke and my child still needed milk. I had to leave her for a couple of days every two weeks and never earned any money, so I asked Pak Thomas to arrange a little payment for me. He was the one who was taking care of Kalpataru's office in Pangkalan Bun.

In 1994, I went with eleven friends of mine to Palang-karaya to get education as a guide and to get a licence. We spent about one month there. Only eight people finally managed to get a licence. There were only two girls and the other guides came from Java. No one else is Dayak and as a woman it's very difficult. I work among the men, and they're very mean sometimes. They put low eyes to me. They say, ah, I'm a woman, I cannot do something like this. Then I want to prove to them that I am able to do the same as them.

I worked for several more months and I only got paid when I escorted guests. I was getting bored asking my boss. I realized that he denied his promises, so I quit and started work with Alam Tours, picking guests up at the airport. I made better money and I started to save some. We have a tourist information service in the airport and there I would go and wait for lost tourists who needed my help. I bought milk and small presents for Karina. She used to say, "Mami, bring me candy and fruit, ya?" When I was away in the forest she would sleep with her grandparents, but when I came back she would never let me go for a second.

Now, being a guide, I felt I could become another person.

In the airport, whenever I met tourists, I'd invite them to come into the tourist information centre, a small lime-dusty room with a pair of wooden chairs and a table. On the wall was a poster of three orphaned orang utans known as Agustin, Purwasih and Tata, who lived peacefully at Camp Leakey, the third ranger-station of the national park. Another poster showed two Dayak men performing a war dance in a longhouse.

While I handed them a guest-book to be signed, I offered my services as a guide to the park or even into remote Dayak areas upriver. I told them my fee was 30,000 rupiah a day (about $15).

Most tours would be to Tanjung Puting, staying at the Rimba Lodge which is owned by Mrs. Birute Galdikas and Charlotte Grimm, but sometimes we slept on a kelotok, or riverboat, which is what I liked best. Nature close. When everything was decided, we'd take a taxi to the police station for permits to enter the park. To speed up the process, we normally handed the typist some cigarette money, otherwise we'd spend a whole day waiting while the typist walked to and fro aimlessly pretending to look for a stamp or a pen.

My new boss at Alam Tours, Pak Katsu, lived in Bali. He was half Japanese, half Dayak. His father had married a beautiful Dayak girl when the Japanese troops were still in Indonesia in the war times. His father fled back to his country when the Japanese lost and left behind his wife and his little boy. Later on, when the boy turned into a man, he went searching and found his father. He stayed in Japan, married a Japanese woman, then started a business in Bali.

I worked with a manager named Apri from Palangkaraya. When we met he was nice, but whenever we had new guests he kept them for himself and told me I was a trainee and had no rights yet. I said to him that I had been working a long time for Kalpataru. I said, "What's different?" But he tried to block every step I made. He was my supervisor because he had a higher position, but I couldn't get along with him because he never gave me any chance to take guests to the jungle. So I got no money. I had a little salary but it was only 150,000 rupiah a month. I went to the office every day; it was my duty to clean the office. I think he didn't like me because I kept asking him when I could go to the forest. I said, "But I can go with you, be like your assistant."

"Oh," he said, "it's only one or two guests, so I don't need assistance."

When I did finally get to go to the forest my job was very easy — giving snacks to guests, making tea, coffee, that's all. All the main duties were carried out by the tour leader, the guide. I never got paid. The boss gave Apri a little money for expenses and told him to share it with me, but he didn't. He kept saying I was in training.

My boss was very rich but he was holding his money tight. Making so much salary, he didn't care and we didn't have any other travel agencies then. Finally Apri went out of town, to Palangkaraya where we had some guests waiting. There was no other guide in the office.

Then some guests booked before he came back, but he said, "Don't ever take guests by yourself because you can destroy our company. You're still in training." Apri told me to find another guide, but I took them to the jungle myself. Then I met him on the way! He stopped our speedboat and started shouting at me, "I told you! Why are you doing this! Look, don't have the guests sit in the back! Let them stay in front so they can see!" It was embarrassing. I had asked them before, but they didn't want to sit in front. After that I hated him, because he embarrassed me. I told my boss about this. I said, "He should not embarrass me in front of the guests." He asked the supervisor to apologize to me, but after that, our relationship was not really good.

There was a problem in the agency over money. My supervisor didn't hand in his receipts. He said, "You know, I never use money for myself, I never touch the money." But when I went to the jungle, Apri kept asking guests for various payments. He said it went to lectures or special tours. He said it was for faxing, for this or that. I believed him, but then I found out that the money went to his pocket.

When I realized that he was playing with the money, I also found out that he was changing my reports. So I kept the originals. Then, before I could report him to my boss, he said that he was going to fire me!

I said, "Oh? Good!" And I wrote a letter saying that I quit, put it on the table, and went home.

I began taking guests into the jungle as a freelance guide. I started to make money again. Less than a month later I got a letter saying that Apri had been fired and asking me to replace him. So I moved back to Alam Tours. For two weeks I worked there alone, doing everything. I think I managed quite well. When I was typing, I sat in the same chair where

Apri sat before! I was smiling. One day he came to pick up some of his things and his face turned red and then pale to see me sitting in his chair, crossing my legs and smiling in a friendly way to him. He turned his face and was gone.

But it didn't last. I worked for two months and then one of the workers in Bali tried to get bad words about me to my boss there. He said the company was losing profits because I was running expenses up. My boss yelled at me and said terrible, insulting things. Like, "Bugger!" Or, "Do you want to make me bankrupt?" He said, "If you don't apologize to me, I can fire you."

In the morning I left. I found out that they wanted to blacklist me, so I wouldn't be able to enter the forest at all.

After that, I moved back to Kalpataru. Their big office was still in Jakarta and they asked if I wanted to be an official guide, on the payroll, not in training any more. When I worked with them, I got my letter — as an official tour guide.

13

To Leave for Ever

I T WAS ABOUT THAT TIME that I met a sailor. He liked to tie up his boat in front of our house. His office was there too, so that's how we met each other. I didn't pay attention to him at first because he was old. We talked to each other, but several months passed before we got closer. He was forty-two. He said he was a widower and that he had two grown-up children. I didn't love him, but I needed a friend to talk to. And we got along; he often visited me.

Karina was also happy with him. My parents didn't really like him, because they said it was bad that I was seeing an old man. And he was Muslim although he said he wanted to change his religion to be mine.

For several months we had a good relationship. Then he said, "I want to marry you." I said, "I don't know if I love you or not, but I need a certificate for Karina's birth. She needs it to enter school."

He said it was okay. He agreed to that. We went to my brother Eby's house in the transmigration area. We met a priest there and asked him about marrying us.

We came to the priest's house in the morning, and said we wanted to be married because Karina needed a certificate so nobody would harrass her that she has no father. I didn't know a priest could marry us without any papers. He just said, "Okay, you're married." And we were. Then he changed that man's religion to be Christian. He asked us to kneel down on the floor and he came with his wife, who had a basin and a flask of water, and he baptised the man. He began the ceremony. I had done nothing. But suddenly he was saying, "Now you are husband and wife." When I think about it, I want to kill myself. It was just so fast.

After that, we came up to my brother's house, and the old man said, "That was a bit quick to change my religion!"

I said, "You wanted it, didn't you?"

He said, "No! The truth is I didn't know what the priest was doing to me." Then he said, "Oh, I hate it. Tonight I want to read the Koran!" The priest had said it was a marriage even though there was no letter. He had a record, but not signed by us, and no pictures, but he said we were legally married. We went back to my brother's and packed our things. The trip home was two hours by bus. When we arrived it was night and he had a message from his boss to take the boat to Java. He said, "I don't have any money. Can you lend me some?" I gave him some money, he went to the boat, and I had no news from him for two months.

My younger sister was complaining. She said, "Why did you do this? Why get married to that man?" She was trying to find out about him and she discovered that he wasn't a widower. He had two official wives and a big bunch of children. He had actually married eleven times! But only two wives were left. The others he had divorced.

He married every place he ever went. And the last place: to me. I'm the twelfth! I thought, what have I done? It was really a mistake. I wrote to him and said, Don't ever dare to come back. But he came. He read my letter and came to my house, but I didn't want to accept him. At that time, I was getting better at my job. I was taking guests out quite often. But he came to my house when I was there and Karina was happy to see him. If I tried to hold her back, she'd cry and call him. I said, "Why did you come here? What do you want?"

I think my family was happier with him. They tried to advise me, but I said, "No, I don't want him any more." I threatened my parents that if they ever allowed him to come into the house, I would move out with Karina and they knew I meant it. The old man kept a little distance then, but he still tried to see us. I always shut the door and I never let Karina come close to him because he tried to use her to come after me.

Then I met a German who was staying in a priest's house in Pangkalan Bun. I took him around town but not to the forest. Actually, I want to forget this story, but sometimes it haunts me. I met Werner a couple of months after the accident of being married to the old sailor who had wives in every harbour he visited. He was nice at first but unfortunately always talked about how much money he had in the bank or in the hand. Still, I needed to escape from the old sailor. What I thought was: I have to move as far away as possible, where he will not be able to reach me.

Nobody knows the guilt that has haunted me about that. I didn't love the German, but I saw him as a small hole to escape through, whatever the risk. So I was showing him around town. It gave me a chance to put some distance between me and that older man. I said, "I have a friend, don't come over. He's better and younger." And the old sailor got so embarrassed he almost stopped speaking, but he still kept trying to get Karina to be close with him again.

One evening the German asked me to join him going to West Kalimantan. I was nervous and talked to my sister about the plan. She said if I thought that was the only way to escape the sailor then to do it. But she said, "Just don't come back crying and saying that things didn't turn out as you expected." I said, "Okay, but don't let our parents know about this."

Werner said we'd just be gone about two weeks. He told me he wanted to get his visa extended. He needed to go to Malaysia for that.

I said, "If you pay everything for my room, for my food, I can go." I couldn't pay. But it was an escape.

I wrote a letter to my parents and wrote a letter to the old man and said: *I have another and don't follow me. I'm going to leave for ever.* I put the letter in my cupboard so my parents couldn't see it. I bought a bag, and I left it at my friend's house. Almost every day, I went there. Every day, I put just one or two things in my little bag, to be ready. So nobody ever suspected my plan. Werner flew to West Kalimantan and I had to fly to Pontianak and he would pick me up at the airport. At the time I was very nervous because the sailorman had anchored his boat to the pier in front of our house.

In a week I had moved all my things. The night before I left I met the sailor in front of the small path to the house and I did not look at him but Karina saw him and ran to him. "Om kep! Om kep!" she shouted joyfully. It means Uncle captain. But I grabbed her and held her. The sailor tried to reach Karina and told me she wanted to be with him. I got mad and said that we had nothing to do with him and I didn't want to see Karina with him. I told him I hated him for trapping me in a terrible marriage.

The night before I left, I put the letter in the cupboard. I had held Karina in my arms all night long. To see her sweet pretty little face broke my heart, but I had to go. My head was blunt. In the morning I arranged my backpack and told my parents I was going to escort some guests to the jungle. I had booked the plane ticket and put a different name on it. I tried to be normal even though my heart was beating hard. I held Karina and tried not to cry as my family would suspect my plan. Karina held onto my neck and talked to me with her sweet child voice, telling me not to be too long and to bring back a present for her. I smiled and told her not to be naughty.

I rented a ride on a motorbike and on the way to the airport I passed a neighbour who asked where I was going. I said, "To the jungle, taking a guest." When I got to the airport, my friends there asked the same question and I said I was waiting for a guest coming on a later flight. My flight was delayed for three hours and I was very nervous as my parents would find the letter and rush to the airport and stop me. When my flight finally came, I took my bag and one of my friends noticed this and was surprised and asked where I was going and I said to Pontianak. He thought I must be joking. I said goodbye to him and walked out to the small plane on the runway. He was standing speechless as I entered the plane. I squeezed myself into the seat and tried to make myself smaller. I felt people's eyes on me, then I felt my own burden fall as the plane took off. High in the sky. I left my family, my job and my little Karina behind. I closed my eyes and felt how tired I was. I crossed my arms as the air was getting cold and the plane was bumping. There were only nine seats — nine passengers — and no one was talking as the cold air soaked into our bones. After one and a half hours on the shaking, small plane we landed in the airport which was very quiet and small. I came out last and I saw Werner by the fence waiting and waving his hand. I smiled and waved back. He said he'd been waiting there since early morning. We got my bag and walked from the airport to the main street and caught a *bemo* to the town. As night fell we went to the bus station and caught a bus. We were going to a small town named Singkawang. Four hours journey. I was planning to stay one week. But I didn't. I stayed longer. I couldn't face going back. Because I was running away with a man, for my family it was very shaming.

I know my way was wrong. I was running away with a man who was not my husband. I would destroy my family's name.

My father tried to find where I was. He didn't believe what I said in my letter. I said, *I want to go far away*, I didn't name the place. *Please, just take care of Karina*, I said. *I may never come back.*

When my mother read the letter, she was crying a lot. My father tried to find me, wherever. He went to every travel agent, to my office, to my friend's house thinking maybe I was hiding there. Finally, they found out the information from the plane's agent. They found out that I went to Pontianak. They said, "Did you see a woman with very long hair?" Because I had changed my name, that's how they identified me.

From Pontianak, the German and I made a four-hour journey. He said he was going to be staying in the Catholic compound. We arrived at midnight. The compound was already quiet as we stepped in, but a Batak girl named Lena was working as head of the boarding house and she greeted us and let me stay in her room. So I went with her and slept there while Werner went to his own room in the corner of the compound. The place was run by a German lady who had married a local Chinese man. She opened the boarding house for orphans and children who came from remote Dayak areas who wanted to study. There were hundreds of children living there. Some were very young. Werner knew the owner because a priest told him about the place. That's the way he travelled in Indonesia. He always tried to find a priest or pastor or people with close links to the church so he could save some money. According to Werner these people do not have the heart to refuse someone who needs a place to stay. That is how he always managed to stay where he got free roof and free food. So he used them for his own benefit. He had no special connection to any church.

Lena took care of the house. She wasn't married and was quite good looking but what I saw was that she was a bit lazy and childish. The boys loved to tease her by throwing lizards at her. She would scream and run tumbling to her room. I decided to stay a little longer with the German. I stayed there almost half a month. I slept a couple of nights in Lena's room, but Werner asked the owner to let me stay in the empty room upstairs because I complained that Lena did not even talk to me or let me climb in her bed. At first, for the first couple of weeks, he was a very nice person. Very nice. He was forty-one, but he looked like thirty.

One day he took me to a big pottery place in the suburbs. It was owned by a Chinese family and there were many men busy making pots. They knead the clay and shape it on round equipment. There was some beautiful pottery in the show-room as well. We went there and one man escorted us around. Werner asked me to choose a pot which he said was to be a present for the man who was taking care of his visa. I chose a small jar with a brown dragon emerging on one side and a blue dragon on the other. We went afterwards to the immi-gration house and met with the man and his wife. We handed over the jar which was wrapped nicely. The next morning we packed our bags and left. Our destination was Lanjak village on the border of Malaysia and West Kalimantan, which would take a couple of days by bus and boats. At the time I was suffering from riding on the bus and got sick and threw up all the time. After a long trip we finally arrived in the small town of Sintang. We spent the night in a small hotel where there were two beds in one room. I had my own bed but he came and slept next to me. He started to kiss me and touch me. I tried to refuse but I thought about the sailorman who claimed that I was his and I got so sick remembering that for the first time I let Werner make love to me. I tried to forget the sailor and kept saying to myself that he never owned me and my body was only mine. The thought made me feel better. It was the first time I had made love to a Western man. At the moment I was scared as my friends used to tell me that making love to a Western man would hurt badly and no Indonesian woman could handle it. My friends said it would be like a grilled fish from down there up to the stomach as the men are all huge.

Later, as we packed, I felt all my bones were crushed and painful under my stomach. I tried to walk normally when we paid for the room as the boys' eyes were stuck on me. We took a public bus to continue the journey. We arrived at a small village by afternoon and found a small floating inn by the Kapuas River. We got one sharp smelly dusty room which was obviously seldom used. I unpacked my bag and took my toothbrush and soap and slipped outside to the rear of the hotel where there was a floating toilet. I bathed in the river using a plastic dipper to pour water on my soapy body. After that I put on a sarong and went back to the room. Werner was already waiting and led me to the small restaurant in front. They served delicious river food such as big shrimps, fishes and chicken at a cheap price. When we ate, Werner got angry because he thought I was playing with the rice and always left some on my plate. He was a high-tempered man and I thought a very high-nosed German. Along the way of our journey he complained about the service and always thought the people tried to get close to him because of his money. He didn't want to talk to the local people who asked him curiously where he was from so I sometimes answered their questions. Now we finished our dinner and moved back to our room. That night he tried to touch me but I put aside his hand. In the morning we continued our journey on a small longboat cruising up the river. On the boat we met with two men. One was the son of the Lanjak village chief. He invited us to stay in his house. The boat cruised the yellowish river, passing numerous small Dayak villages before entering a remote and huge lake. It was beautiful and took some hours to cross. We arrived at night in Lanjak village, whose aromas of wet soil met my nose as we got off the boat carrying our heavy backpacks.

The chief's house was simple with high stilts like most of the village houses. We were greeted by his father, a middle-aged man of fifty who spoke English fluently. He showed us a room at the rear of the house and his sister prepared a mattress for us and a pillow. The next room was for his son and his friend and the other man who was already there. We stayed two days. For lunch we went to the small *warung* in the village where the woman who owned it said all her food came in from Malaysia. They were using rupiahs and ringgit as well. Werner gathered some information about a cave high in the mountain which he intended to visit. The woman said that the cave was difficult to get to and only bat hunters knew about the place. It was covered by fog and the path was closed by wilderness. We decided not to go there as the mountain was very high and dangerous.

One morning the son of the chief invited us to visit his friend in a Dayak Iban village. We walked a couple of hours up and down the red soil road made by the timber company. By midday we saw the longhouses which stood in the distance. We went to the large one in the middle which was very old and made of ironwood. It was long and separated into rooms. The difference between the longhouses in our tribe and this longhouse was that it had a room for each family and a long veranda along the side where the people conduct most of their daily activities such as weaving baskets or weaving the beautiful expensive cloths on small, traditional looms. This Dayak Iban tribe's language was so different from mine that I only understood a few words. They have more slanting eyes and light skin as well and tattoos all over their bodies which do not exist in our tribe. They use a needle and Chinese ink to make the traditional tattoos. They stick the needle in the skin hundreds of times until the ink is absorbed and stays in the skin. The tattoos would hurt and be swollen for weeks. The Iban mostly have tattoos around the throat and hands or feet depending on their status in the community. The son of the chief took us to the last room and introduced us to a Western man. He was in his mid-thirties and he'd been staying there for some years already, studying the culture. He spoke Iban fluently and I could hardly tell that he was not a native Dayak to hear him talking. He invited us for lunch with fern vegetables and fragrant rice. Then he took us behind the longhouse, where we entered a small lush forest and ended our walk by a small waterfall. The water was jumping from a height of at least four metres and was very beautiful. I picked up a brown flower of tengkawang from the wet ground and threw it to the air. The flower rolled slowly and beautifully like a helicopter before it landed, reminding me of my childhood.

Later, we followed him to the jungle. Werner was complaining all the way and grumbled that he understood nothing. He didn't even know where the other man was leading us. I kept quiet and followed the man up the small path, passing small streams and old ladangs before arriving at a palm plantation. A local man climbed one of the palm trees and took a middle-sized bamboo cylinder down. I understood finally that the palm juice could be made into palm wine when mixed with a certain root. They let it stand overnight and by the next morning it changes to strong wine. I understood that we had come for a jungle rice-wine party. I tasted a little and it was sharp and bitter. Werner kept grumbling and refused the offer of wine. One man suddenly pointed his airgun at a tree and shot a pygmy squirrel that was cornered and trying to escape. After more than five shots the small squirrel fell down and they burned the hair before peeling off the delicate skin, taking out the intestines and baking it on a small fire. They offered us some as they divided the squirrel meat which was no bigger than a mouse. I did not take any as the meat was too little. They drank a lot and when the afternoon fell, we were led back to the village and said goodbye to the Western man whose name I forget.

We spent some days in the Lanjak chief's house before continuing on our journey. Werner wanted to go to Putussibau town but people told him that the road was too bad so he changed his destination and we went to Badau village which was one hour from the border of Malaysia. The Iban people in this village shop in Malaysia as it is closer than Pontianak. They carry big rattan backpacks off in the mornings and come back in the late afternoons with heavy loads of salt, sugar and biscuits. As in Lanjak, they use both rupiahs and ringgit. When we shopped for our daily needs, they gave us small change in ringgit coins which later we could not use in other places. We stayed for two days and went on to a small village named Kekura far away in the mountains. We went there by truck and arrived in the late afternoon, going to a longhouse that was 150 metres in length and occupied by hundreds of people, men, women and children. One man invited us for dinner and they prepared mattresses and pillows. We slept on the floor by the veranda. In the morning we bathed in a small clear river behind the longhouse. When we came back from bathing, many people had already gathered and stared curiously at us. Werner used the chance to take pictures and some of the men proudly showed their tattoos which covered most of the exposed parts of their bodies. Flower, animal, dragon and abstract motifs painted on the bare upper body as well as the thigh and further down. That day we arranged for a local guide who would take us to the waterfall in the mountains. We departed after breakfast.

After about an hour we began climbing. Our guide told us people seldom visited this waterfall as it was far away and dangerous. I was very tired and moved slowly, grabbing small plants to help me keep my balance. In the middle of the hill I almost could not continue and grabbed at a small plant whose root was too shallow to hold my weight and came out suddenly. I felt the blood rush to my feet as I lost my balance. My eyes darkened and I blindly grabbed at every bit of green I saw and luckily grabbed a strong one. I pressed myself to the ground. My heart was pounding and my knees were weak. I looked down and suddenly got dizzy as I saw how high I was. I didn't see Werner as he had left me and was far above, but I moved when I heard him call me. I don't know how long we had been climbing but the weather was getting worse and without warning the clouds suddenly gathered and within moments a heavy rain poured over us. We kept walking as we could hear the sound of the waterfall getting closer. Finally we arrived at an open area and in front of us a very tall waterfall jumping like it was pouring from the sky. People in the village say it is higher than the pakit tree and the pakit is the highest tree in the jungle. I was shaking. The mountain air was cold. I searched through the mud on my body for leeches and found some that were fat from sucking my legs. Werner was busy taking pictures with his small automatic camera. We followed our guide climbing the side of the waterfall where there were levels and every level had a pool. I thought I was almost a hundred metres high. We spent almost an hour there before leaving. Going down was faster but the trail was very slippery. That evening we washed ourselves in the river and after dinner fell fast asleep.

14

Too Heavy to Carry

I DIDN'T WRITE ANY LETTERS to my family to tell them where I was.

We went to many small villages, then tried to arrange transportation back to Badau but the owner of the house where we were staying wanted fifteen thousand rupiah to rent us his motorbike. I was embarrassed as this German man complained and rudely picked up his backpack and left the house. I tried to say goodbye to the people there as they had given us food and a place to stay, but I suddenly realized what kind of man I was dealing with. It was too late to regret. After a long walk we got a ride on a truck to Badau village.

The next morning we got a truck to take us back to Lanjak and the following morning back to Singkawang town. In Singkawang we stayed for more weeks before taking a passenger ship to Jakarta. We took the economy class and we chose a place by the cafeteria and spread the rental mattresses on the floor. It was very hot in the day time and very windy at night. After a day and a night on the ship we arrived in Tanjung Priok harbour. When we stepped off the ship, a young man came up and suddenly opened the zipper on Werner's backpack. Upset, I warned him. The man looked at me angrily and moved away very fast.

We spent a week in Jakarta. The place where we stayed was called Jalan Jaksa where most budget-conscious travellers gathered. It was hot and busy. Every time we were out, my eyes were wandering everywhere. There were lots of new things — the night women on the street, school-aged and beautiful, the gays kissing and holding each other, all the things I have not seen in my hometown. It made me depressed and I wanted to go home. After a week we moved down to Jogyakarta, then to Pacitan in east Java where we stayed by the beach in a bunga-low owned by an Australian who married an Indonesian. After a few days we moved to the beach at Pangandaran in west Java where we explored the national park with its wild buffalo and deer. Werner lent me his snorkel and told me how to use it. It was very impressive. I put on the mask and stood with the coral under my feet and put my head under water and everything was so beautiful. I almost drifted away in the wave because I was so excited and floated with the current. I never saw coral in Kalimantan. Afterwards, we continued our trip to Surabaya then to Bali.

We stayed at Kuta in Bali for four days before continuing the trip to Lombok and stayed at Gilimeno island which is very famous for the snorkelling area with its blue coral. From

Gilimeno we continued to Flores visiting the hot spring, the beach with its beautiful coral. In Flores I was almost killed by the sea once. I was too excited to see the coral and I ignored the warning not to go far from shore. Close to the beach the coral was most broken from earthquakes so I moved slowly and the further out I got, the more beautiful the coral was and suddenly I realized that the shore was too far away. I tried to swim back but there was a strong undercurrent sucking me further out to sea. Werner reached me and dragged me by the hand to the shore. I was out of breath and I sat on the sand and was upset for quite a while.

In Flores we also visited the Three Colours Lake in Meno, down from Ende. Once we visited the priest and asked whether we could marry there but the answer was no because the paper was not easy, especially if it has something to do with a foreigner. We moved down to Labuhan Bajo and stayed in Caci island where a German girl who married a Lombok man had opened a small resort. The place was beautiful and romantic. It was a small island about twenty minutes from Labuhan Bajo. Everyday I went snorkelling and I could spend hours floating on the water watching seaporcupines or hundreds of small fishes by the coral. One morning I went snorkelling alone and saw an octopus as big as a fruit bowl with spreading arms more than one metre in length. I was so excited watching him. When he felt disturbed he became darker. At first I was surprised by the change and looked up from the water thinking there was a problem with my snorkel glasses. Then I found out that the octopus itself changed colour amazingly. At last I came out of the water, freezing and as pale as a dead body. A couple of days later we went back to Surabaya by night bus. We stayed for some days in Surabaya and tried to get ship tickets back to Pontianak, because Werner still had to finalize his visa. He had to go to Malaysia and Pontianak was the cheapest and closest way.

I noticed that he tried to get close with an Arabian lady on the ferry from Lembar to Bali. My good feeling for him faded little by little, but at least I did not have to think about the old sailor. Werner never owned my body; I am the owner of my body. That thought made me feel better. In Surabaya we quarrelled and he showed his sour face all the time. I felt something would happen. When we were on the ship I got very sick and could not get up and lay on the row bed in the economy class which smells of people's vomit and stale food. I was too sick to get up but he would not help to get me some food. I finally had to get up from my hunger. I walked slowly and he talked harshly to me as he thought I was moving too slowly down the hall to the pantry. Suddenly I hated him. I could not stand his arrogant manner. We quarrelled again. I dreamed that Karina drowned and I tried to grab her, but failed.

Before the announcement telling us that we were close to the harbour of Banjarmasin in South Kalimantan and would be stopping over before continuing the journey to Pontianak, I suddenly got the idea of stopping in Banjarmasin and going down to Pangkalan Bun. I told Werner about it. I told him that I had had a bad feeling for some days and in the night always dreamed about Karina. I worried that something had happened to her. I'd left her for more than three months already and I worried that she was sick.

I prepared my things and Werner loaned me his small bag as mine was too heavy to carry. He gave me some money and said it was to buy a ticket to Pontianak after I met my family. I did not suspect anything and took the money. He gave me a little more for paying for my transportation home. It was very little and I had to be careful as the money was only enough to pay for the longboat down to Palangkaraya where my sister lived and later on I had to take a bus to my town. I went down to the ship and he escorted me to the gate. We took the *ojek* on the street. It was a rental motorcycle and we had to bargain for a good price. He kissed my cheek, said goodbye and turned around, leaving me alone by the harbour. It was four o'clock in the morning.

The journey usually takes four to five hours depending on the tide. If we're lucky we can get a high tide which means we will not be stuck and delay our journey for a day. That's why people depart early in the morning. The boat I took was a longboat with an engine. It has a plastic tent roof which protects the passengers from rain or heat. I paid 22,000 rupiahs for one way. We passed many small villages and lush forest along the winding river. I loved the journey. I loved all the green with monkeys sometimes jumping in the trees. I saw tingang, the hornbill, our holy bird flying low making its laugh-like sound. How I missed the jungle, the place where I used to work, the orang utan, the other guides and rangers and boatmen — my friends. I was thinking that I'd been away too long. I was tired. I wanted to settle down somewhere and not to have to move all the time. To be with my friends who used to share stories and always laughed a lot. With Werner I had to be serious. I always thought it must have something to do with his age. He was only a few years younger than my father. He used to talk about the money he owned in the bank. We quarelled every time he insulted me by saying that I come from a poor family. I answered him, "Do not say bad things about my family. I'm proud of them and I don't think you come from a rich family, do you?" Our friendship was worse since we'd come back from Lombok. When I did not understand what he said he would look at me and say, "You don't know this word?" as if I was really stupid. And I some-times really didn't know what he meant as his English gram-mar was even worse than mine! He used to tell people when he met them, proudly, that he learned his English from his friends in the military compound. He learned and picked up words from them. I said in my heart, "Ugh, that's why your English is not better," but I never said it out loud.

My journey to Palangkaraya was longer than I expected. The boat had engine trouble. Once my mamah had told me that when a member of her family died anywhere along the Kahayan River, the body would be taken by longboat down to Pahandut village, which is now Palangkaraya. The journey was slow and sometimes, when Kambe — the bad spirit — caught up with them, he sat on the dead person and made the longboat too heavy to move. Then one of the men on the boat would load his handmade gun and fire it at the sky. The spirit would be frightened away, and so it would go — the boat stopping, the gun firing all the way to the village.

This time we were lucky because our engine trouble started during a stopover and the driver told us to go on by road. He arranged a public bemo to take us to Palangkaraya, which was not far away, but I was the last one and did not get a seat, so I stayed a little longer and finally the driver stopped a pickup and asked them to take me. There were two men in front — a Chinese-like man and his friend. I sat between them. On the way I told them that I was going to Palangkaraya to visit my sister, Arita. They did not believe me and thought that I was Javanese. Many women from Java work as night girls there. I said that I was Dayak. They said, "If you are Dayak and your family come from this area, do you know these people?" and they mentioned some familiar names to me.

I said, "Of course I know him and he is my uncle."

But they did not give up and asked again, "Do you know Rahen's family in this town?"

I could not hold my smile any more and said, "Did you know that she is my grandma? They are my mamah's parents."

One of the men was very surprised and laughingly said that he was one of the Rahen family. I found out later that he was my uncle! There is no wonder that my mamah sometimes told us that we come from a big family that has lived in the province of Central Kalimantan for a long time. They've spread all over since a long time ago. Since Palangkaraya was still named Pahandut village.

The journey was very pleasant and they escorted me to the centre of the town. All the way we did not talk with Bahasa Indonesia but with our own Bahasa Kapuas, my mother's language. I arrived in the night at my sister's house. I held her tightly and could not stop my tears.

15

This Gold Bracelet

WERNER WAS ON HIS WAY to Pontianak and I was with my two sisters in Palangkaraya — Lilis was staying with Arita. I spent the night and the next morning took a bus down to my town. It was a day's journey on muddy and unasphalted roads. My younger sister Lilis came with me as she got her holiday so we could go back together and when we arrived in my town, I asked her to go home first and not to tell my parents about my presence. I wasn't ready to meet them. So I went to the market and wandered around. After about an hour I went to my home. Just as I entered the house my sister, Yayang, came out and held me. She was the one who helped me with my plan to go to Kalimantan.

Then a small child came running into the living room. My goodness, she was so pretty! She came and held me and hid her smile. Her face was joyful. I held her and kissed her.

I lifted her. She was so light and skinny. I let tears run down my cheeks. My throat was aching and I could not say anything. Karina did not want to move from me and she happily opened the present I'd bought in Palangkaraya. She was laughing and talking a lot. How I'd abandoned my little baby! Later on, my mamah told me that the sailor had left. She said they never saw him any more. I felt like a stone had been lifted from my chest.

The next day I received a telegram from Werner. My feeling warned me, but I opened the envelope and I was shocked. It said that by the time I received it, he would not be in Pontianak any more and was probably already in Malaysia. He asked me not to go to Pontianak as he would not be there. He said, *I send all your clothes, with your bag now. I'm sorry, because I want to go to Malaysia very fast. I'm not coming back so don't come. Here are your clothes.*

Finished.

I tried to call him several times and finally I reached him in the house of the owner of the compound. He was still there. But what he said by telephone made me feel worse. He said, "I spent lots of money on you, and I don't want to be with you any more. You live in your own world, and I live in my own world, so we are different. We cannot stay together. Just forget me, and live in your own world, and I will live in mine. Don't make any phone calls to me."

I was very shocked because he was talking about food he bought for me and it meant he did not do it willingly. It was as if he was taking back the food from my mouth that he given me. Every time I thought about that I wanted to kill him and take his stomach out. I said, "Why did you promise like this, like this, before?" I felt sick.

I remembered our long journey together. Mostly we were visiting caves. And climbing mountains. I'd had a good time with him. For a while I'd felt better. I asked him to marry me because we were already together and I was a woman staying with a man and not being married. We went to several places, in Java and also in Bali trying to find a small church where they would marry us, but it couldn't happen. They always asked for our baptismal letters and our parents' permission to be married.

After a month or two, he wasn't kind any more. He would insult me. He said, "You cannot behave yourself in the city."

For instance, when we went into a store sometimes, I didn't know how to go to the lift — I mean escalator. I didn't know how. I had to watch first. And I had a problem with buses. When I rode on one, I always got sick. I'd throw up everything. Every time. I kept asking him not to go by bus. I said it's okay by motorbike or by car, but please not by bus. When I even heard about a bus, I already wanted to throw everything up.

I was with him for about three and a half months. But I don't regret it. I'll never regret it. Because of him, I managed to release myself from that older man.

I went back to my work, taking guests to the jungle. My spirit slowly came alive again. But I knew inside my feeling was changed. It's always difficult for me to trust a man. But I enjoyed life among my friends and worked as hard as possible so I could save money. No one ever asked my story, which helped me a lot to recover. I tried to dig for any feelings that I might like somebody, but the feeling was hard to find.

In our country, it's *very* difficult to find a man who would accept me with my experience. He would dig out all the things that ever happened. It's complicated. I'm imprisoned here, so I try not to think about my life before. Still, sometimes when I'm alone, I think, it's not right! But I think the best thing I ever did was to throw the older man away. I keep telling myself I didn't even marry him. That it wasn't legal. It was a mistake. So I keep telling myself. . . .

Sometimes my friends ask me why I'm not married yet. You're going to be thirty! they say. And when you're thirty, nobody wants you. Think about your little daughter. She needs a father, not just a mother. She needs balance in her life.

The truth is that half a year after Werner left, I met someone else. He was in a big group but he was travelling with his mother. Shawn was twenty-nine years old and bearded. He had very light skin and was handsome. I fell in love with him. My feeling was cold and he made it warm. He talked about how lucky I was to live in the jungle. His mother was a tall, mid-forties woman and must have been beautiful when she was young. Shawn told me that his mother married when she was still a very young girl. That was why their age difference wasn't too great. I did not think his mother liked me at the time because Shawn always tried to be with me. The tour group was using two boats and Shawn would see which boat I was going to be on and join me.

We spent four days in the jungle. In the afternoon, after

coming back from the camp, we took a canoe and led the guests to see proboscis monkeys and birds by the riverside. Shawn joined my canoe. Each canoe had two people so I was alone with him. We talked about many things until he told me that the next day he had to leave. While we talked we did not realize that the current had become strong and was taking our boat downstream. We had to paddle back to the hotel as our boat had passed the first park station. The last night I was sitting on the hotel pier with Shawn and his friend, Adam, and Scott, our tour leader, having an after-dinner conversation. Most of the guests had gone to their rooms because the flight was early the next morning. Slowly Adam and Scott left us alone. Adam joined the boys in the lobby singing. They sang together and suddenly came outside to tease us. We were laughing with each other to see them. They called us love birds.

We got closer and we talked to each other, and then we got closer very fast! We went swimming alone. An American. He lives in Atlanta. He's a photographer. He was so kind. He asked me to be his girlfriend.

Four days. It's really not enough. He said, "When I go back, I'll send you some money, some dollars, then please arrange for your passport. And I can send you a ticket, and you can come. You can arrange everything, come to my place and marry me." And he sent me some money, but I never got a passport because I hadn't told him about my life before. He didn't know that I was married and had Karina.

He sent two hundred dollars. Just to arrange for a passport. I keep the money here, on my arm, so that's why I never spend it. I keep it here. This gold bracelet.

I kept correspondence with him. I finally told him about Karina, my marriage, all my nightmares. He said he was sorry that I had to suffer so much and he wanted to fix it. He kept writing to me but then he found out that it's very difficult to marry in America. He said he's going to come to my parents and ask for me and we can be married here. We were faxing each other every day. I have a big bunch of letters!

He made plans to come in February, 1995. He booked his ticket, it was all arranged. But his boss had an accident; he fell down some stairs, about four metres, and was almost paralyzed. His boss had to sell the company because he couldn't manage it in his condition, so Shawn lost his job. He had to move to his mother's house, in Arizona, and try to find another job. He was planning to come and visit me, but said he needed to find another job first, before he came.

He said he came from a very cold area. That's why they mostly have very pale skin. Atlanta? Something like that. In the coast. Somewhere on the east coast. And it's very, very cold. His father died about four or five years ago. His mother is a pilot — a jet pilot. And she was always moving the family when he was young. He said he's sorry he always moved from one place to another place. He never settled anywhere for a long time. He worked in Atlanta. And then Prescott. He said it's a very nice place, with mountains, but it's really hot.

He had a hard time. He was working on a farm, just for food and rent. His letters got slowly, slowly reduced. One month apart, then two months, and finally no letters at all. He sent his last letter September, 1995. When I had my birthday, he sent me a fax, that's all.

I have lots of pictures of him. He sent me many pictures. Pictures of Atlanta — lots of nice trees, waterfalls. . . . And I sent him pictures. Many kinds. Every time I sent a letter to him, I put in pictures. Now I have no news, no nothing. I made a phone call to his mother once, but she wasn't in. And the call was expensive! It was the phone number where she works. He didn't give me any phone number for her house.

When we were in the jungle he said to me, "Riska, I like you. You are very special and you are very lucky to live next to the jungle." For me it was funny because I thought he was the lucky one to live in a Western prosperous country where there is no starving and stupidity. Here we have to struggle for our life. We have to work hard to get a plate of rice. The white people working with us here, they would get a tremendous payment because they speak English and come from Europe even though they know nothing. But our workers who have better knowledge are willing to work hard and are more qualified than those white workers, only get poor payment which amounts to the cost of one dinner for those white people. It's sad because our people have not yet learned how to appreciate themselves. If an Indonesian worker gets 250,000 rupiah a month, then those foreigners get maybe five or ten times as much for the same position. Very sad. So many people are not satisfied and this causes lots of social jealousy. Our government set up a new law, which has never been practised, that the hotels or companies should not employ more than three foreigners in the future in order to give more chance and experience to the Indonesian worker and to avoid any further social problems. But people think that if we have foreign workers our company is a prestigious one. Every five star hotel or big company always has foreigners in the peak positions.

In Kalimantan I love the atmosphere. When we work, there are no higher or lower people. We are a big family. Often I eat from the same plate as the boatman. Very close. Once, when I worked with Best Tours, which has a head office in Bali, we were taking small groups to Tanjung Puting National Park and there was a guide from Bali and an American tour leader, Mr. Hans. The guide was very arrogant; that's what we thought. He was complaining all the time about the service. He said the workers were not good. I said to him that this was Kalimantan, not Bali, and that was the way people lived here. We did not offer big fake smiles but we shared our lives. He told me not to be close with all the boatmen and rangers and he said I had to show them that I was the one they should respect because I was the guide. Some of the boatmen were annoyed and said that if he couldn't work with the boatmen and the people in the park, he would fail. One of them told me he could strand the boat in floating plants and ruin the tour if that guide behaved rudely. He should respect them and treat them at the same level. We are family and unfortunately most people from outside Kalimantan expect the way we live, our socialization, to be modern. But they do not understand us. We are happy with our way. And I hope it will stay the same.

16

The Only Way

WHEN I WAS IN THE FOREST, Karina slept with my mother. My mother came to our bed and slept with her. But when I came back, she never wanted to sleep with my parents. And one thing: if I went to the forest or anywhere else, I told Karina exactly how many days. She's very smart. Even when she was a baby, she could count, like, a hundred and a hundred. If I said I have to go for four days from Sunday, she would count it: "Okay, Sunday and four days? Okay." If I was late, she would wait, wait and not want to eat, and keep saying, "My mom promised that she will come today."

My mother takes her to church. When I was in junior high school, senior high school, when they had groups or a pageant at Christmas, I tried to participate. But they took mostly the rich and beautiful girls and they never took me.

Shortly after Ahwa left, my sister, Arita, met a young Christian priest in our town who was from the same tribe as my parents. At that time I didn't like this priest and one day I had a fight with him. I said that all the priests were unfair because when they had a chorus or something they only chose the pretty, rich people to have parts. I said it hard. My face was sour and my voice was high as I said all my disappointment. "What kind of church is this where it's always the richest person, the most beautiful person who gets everything?"

At that time I felt terrible about the church, because I thought it was a place for people to show that they have nice clothes and things. And I didn't have anything.

Finally, I met with some friends and we started a vocal group. I was singing. That's the first time I had my own experience in a church. We sang at Christmas and sometimes on Sunday.

When she was nearly two years old, my parents talked to a lady who was a shaman about removing a blue vein on Karina's forehead. It was a bad omen. If a child is born with a bad omen, she could die in the river or be eaten by a crocodile. The lady made a ceremony at my parent's house. I was there too. Karina sat in my parents' lap near the open door. The lady made a fire and burned some sweet-smelling roots. There was rice and praying and mantras. The lady shaman put a needle in the fire then touched Karina's forehead. The vein disappeared.

My parents adore my child. They love her and they don't quite trust me to take care of her. It's a kind of blind love. I was a nursing mother for two years. But maybe it's also good — their love — because I can have my time to go to the jungle and do my work. And they really support me. They support me when I have no work. And my child.

Sometimes Karina says, "Mommy, you don't have to go to the jungle. Stay with me, you never stay with me."

I say, "Karina, I must go, because it's my job."

When I come home, I always bring something for her, like food or fruit. She likes fruit. It cheers her up.

She has lots of friends. It's really amazing to me. For me it's very difficult sometimes to make a friend so fast like that.

She's also really brainy. I think I was lucky. In most things that happen, I'm really lucky because she's growing up to be really nice and clever. Before she entered school she already knew the numbers and all the alphabet. After three months at school she could read and write. My brother, my youngest brother — I'm not really so close with him — said, "Oh, it's amazing that in just three months she can write and read."

My first brother, Eby, went to university for three years and now he is working as a teacher in a senior high school in a transmigration area — where the government sends people from Java to get land for free. First the government clears the area. They take out all the trees with chainsaws. Then it's ready to cultivate. The government gives a fee to them and about one year's help with supplies. Eby is married to a girl from our mother's tribe. She is working as an elementary school teacher. Their small village is called Pangkalan Lada, and it's about two hours from Pangkalan Bun. They have two boys. I always think that they are a happy, small family. They have a small house with high stilts in their small pepper plantation. My brother borrowed money from the bank to build that little house and every month he pays some back, cutting from his salary. My brother loves his plantation. They have a thousand pepper trees and he dreams about buying a colour TV from his first harvest, but they'll have to wait for at least three years.

My second brother, Ouberhand, or Uber, is working in a small town up the river from Palangkaraya, as a forestry policeman. He never atttended university because he got his job right after he finished junior high school, a three-year education following the six years of elementary school. He spent most of his time drinking at the billiard table in town and often did not attend class. Mamah got many reports that my brother was spending his school time in the pool hall. Finally one day she quietly followed him. My brother walked to school with his school uniform — about a half-hour walk. He obviously knew that our mother was sneaking behind him, but he pretended not to know and hesitated at the crossing where he would choose between the road to school or the pool hall. He took the one leading to school, although we don't know if he ever entered that day. After a difficult time, he finally managed to finish his study and luckily in our town the goverment was looking for healthy young people to be trained as forestry police. My brother was trained with some others for six months in what he said was a military system. Once he wrote a sad letter to my parents saying that he almost could not stand it because the coach was too disciplined and too rude. He got kicked by the coach because he ran too slowly. He said his boots were too tight so it hurt to run and he was asking money from my parents to buy new boots.

Although Uber was handsome, his body well muscled and well built, and his skin light, he had difficulty finding a wife. He would love a girl but the girl would not love him. Or a girl would be madly in love with him but he would not love her. It happened all the time. So my parents finally spoke to Bopai Toyo from Delang River, a medicine man, and he told my parents that my brother had to be cleaned because he was under a bad spirit. The medicine man said probably my brother had hurt a woman who was in love with him. And she got her revenge by cursing him with a bad spirit which covered his body so every woman he loved would hate him and he would hate the women who loved him. And he would never manage to get a wife the whole of his life unless he was cleansed.

One day the medicine man arranged a special ceremony for my brother. Young coconut blossoms, which had to be still in bud, and fragrant flowers were included. He told my brother not to use his best underwear because when he bathed him at midnight he should throw away all the things on his body. But regrettably my brother wore his best, expensive underwear and had to throw it away later on. So he was bathed in the night and poured over with rich mantras. And not long after the cleansing, he met a girl from the Dayak Siang tribe who was working in the public health centre. They married in her village in a small wooden church and now they have two baby girls.

Then the third is my sister who works as a teacher in junior high school in Palangkaraya. Her name is Arita, but we call her Ita, mostly. She's married to a Dayak man who teaches in the university and they have three boys.

The fourth is me, Isa. And the fifth is Onny Liesta, but we call her Lilis, who is now graduated after five challenging years in the university in Palangkaraya. She was a biologist but she is now working as a teacher in a small harbour town, Kumai.

The sixth, Leo, the youngest brother, is now grown up, has no job and has stopped his study. He lives with my parents. When he was a baby he got a very high fever and got stiff and unconscious several times. So my parents say that after that he is a little bit out of his mind.

The youngest sister is Yayang. She also gave up her study at the university of Palangkaraya. She loves clothes and is always trying to look stylish. She has light skin and is the prettiest of all of us. She only wants to work and get money.

My parents are really poor because they had to send all their children to school. They cannot make a renovation of our house, they cannot buy things because all the money goes to their children. Mamah mostly supports the family. My brother's old but he gets like a child; he wants to have all attention on him. When somebody is in front of him, he will laugh or make noise so people will notice. If he is around he makes trouble, fighting, asking for money. And if my parents don't give him what he wants, he breaks everything in the house. I think my father loves him, because he is the only son he has who is unmarried, and whatever Leo asks of him, he will give it directly. Once, my father bought him a motorbike with my mother's money. It cost about one million rupiah.

And he sold it for one hundred thousand. Then he wanted a speedboat. And my father bought a speedboat for him. And he sold it for one hundred thousand again!

I remember when Karina was only a week old. My youngest brother threatened to pour boiling water on her and said that he wanted to kill her. He said, "Don't ever make me mad. I can kill your daughter, I can pour boiling water on her."

And one time when I was sitting and nursing my baby, he came to me and hit me on the head. I was so mad.

He hit me in my stomach. He hit my side, and I was sort of dazed and I really meant to kill him then. He went down, and I was holding the table and I grabbed the knife but my sister's boyfriend grabbed me and twisted the knife out of my hand. I'll never forget it.

My mother, I think she was there, but she didn't dare say anything. This brother is always hitting her if she says a little word. I think I hate him for things like fighting my mother. But my father will just say, "Why are you doing this?" as if he blames my mother. He doesn't have any courage.

And I don't like my mamah sometimes, because I want her to fight him back, or ask him to move because he's a grown man.

Sometimes I ask them to get rid of Leo, to tell him to get a job.

And they say, "But what can he do?"

I think Leo doesn't like me because I'm the only person in the house who never wants to do what he says. I have my principles. It's better to fight with him than do what he says.

I wish that my mother had asked him to leave the house. It's their right to be there and all the trouble was just from him, every day. He's never had a job. And he goes to school about once a month. It's university, but it's nothing. No quality. If you just show up sometimes, you can pass.

Another time, not long ago, Karina was sick. She was staying in my parents' room. I was in my room because I was so tired and Karina was sick. I just wanted a little sleep. And he came in to my parents' room and did something that woke my father, and my father started yelling. Then it was like hell.

He was drunk and shouting at my parents and hitting the door where Karina was lying down. He lifted his hand and the door was broken. I was terrified. I always carry my knife when I know that he's around. Karina was two metres from that door! And my parents did nothing to stop it. So I said, "Ask him to stop. Otherwise he'll die." And I had my knife.

My father promised me that Karina would be safe.

If I said to my parents, I have to take Karina away from this house, they would never allow it.

When he's home, which is nearly all the time, the house is always messy. It's terrible. The wall is all broken, the chairs are broken. Just one person in our family spoils everything.

Because I have Karina it's something that makes me worry. I worry about her. I'm not surprised any more if something happens. Really. If somebody's killed, I won't be surprised.

Family. It's often hard to live together and get along.

Karina liked to watch my father playing chess, and one day she asked me to teach her how. I wasn't in a good mood, and I was teaching her, and she was trying to remember the way the horse went. She made a wrong move, and I got mad and shouted.

She didn't cry. She just looked at me and never said anything. No word at all. But I could see her face. It was very red. She went quietly to the corner of our bed, and hid herself under the blanket! I heard her crying. She said, "My mom's very angry with me!"

I don't know what happened to me. I came to her, sat on the bed and held her, and she said, "I don't want to play chess any more! Never, never," she said. "I don't want it. Because," she said, "you always get angry."

After that, when I was teaching her, I tried not to lose my temper. She learned quite well. She saw how my father blocked the rook with the castle and the queen. And soon she was teaching me! "Oh, no," she said, "you must lock this horse. Then just pick it up and move it."

After more than thirty years away, Mamah returned to her village to attend Arita's wedding. I was there and could see how my mamah's mother behaved. I was angry and sad when my mamah came to her after many, many years, after marrying and leaving her village and then finally meeting again with her parents and her ten sisters whom she left when they were still kids and who now had families. My mamah hugged her mother tearfully but her mother just said, "Oh, you're here then," without hugging back. My mamah is a strong lady so she just ignored it. She met her youngest sister for the first time, a sister who was born when she was away. Her youngest sister is a year younger than me. I did not like her because she tried to be the person who got all the attention. When we were together and nobody was around, I called her names that made her furious. She wanted me to call her aunty but I said I was older so there was no need to call her aunty. She told her parents some bad things about me. And her parents, who are also my grandparents, always believed her and blamed me. They said we are no good. My mamah's family did not agree to her marriage, so my sister, who lived and studied there, always got bad treatment and bad words from them. But she was always patient and behaved nicely so she managed to live there. When I entered college (for that short time) and had to live in Palangkaraya, I managed, for a week after my arrival, to refuse my sister's request to visit my mamah's family to be introduced. I said harshly that I would not go there just to get insulted. My sister begged me and said that if I didn't visit them I would wish her trouble in the future. So finally I went with her to visit my aunty and grandparents, whom I had already guessed would not treat me nicely.

When we visited them they just said hi and retreated, leaving us alone. I was hurt and said to my sister that I would not go there any more. They were not nice because we have nothing, that's what I felt. Which is why my mamah never went back even though her heart was full of longing. I can still remember how she told us her childhood stories — how she followed her father catching fishes in the river, she and her oldest sister waking early in the dawn and going to the river with fishing nets and small baskets to collect fishes. They cruised up the river in a wooden canoe. My mamah and her sister would paddle the canoe and her father would stand in the middle looking for a good place to throw his net. He would give a sign to stop when he decided on the place and then hold the net and throw it steadily out to the deeper water. Then, if they were lucky, they'd go back home with a catch. The memory was hard, wet and cold, but sweet. When she was speaking, I could see her eyes looking to the distance, dry and empty. My poor mamah, she had to pass all the misery, leaving her family and her home just to be with my papah. I can see myself sometimes in her. I would do anything if I think it is good for me. Her misery was solid but she passed it all bravely. She is a survivor.

Where to live is a problem for a girl. And how. In my culture, people believe Aaaah! A woman who was once married always wants to go for men. That's the reason I don't want to tell people about my marriage. If I said, "Well, I'm going to go and get an apartment now, or rent a room somewhere...," it's a problem. You have to depend on your family. It's not really nice if a woman lives alone. It's bad for her name. So we seldom live away from home. For a woman, maybe marriage is the only way.

When I was fifteen years old and was falling in love with the Chinese man who lived across the river, I had my periods already. My breasts were full and big and my body was shaping. But my friends at school teased me that I had big breasts and it was embarrassing because people think if a girl has big breasts it means that they are probably being touched by men. So I tried to hide them. I wore a very tight bra and sometimes

I almost could not breathe but my breasts looked small and a little flat and so I was happy.

Once when I was on my way home from school I walked along the main road. The day was hot and I was sweating a lot and there were some men on the other side of the road. One of them crossed the road and suddenly reached out his hand and kneaded my breast. I looked at him and saw his ugly face laughing and I was so angry that tears came down my cheek. Nobody helped and everybody only looked. I was embarrassed and could not do anything.

When I went home, my papah asked me what happened. I told him. He asked what the men looked like and I told him what I remembered and he said it could be some of the people from Madura that were working in the rubber factory. He went out searching for them, fruitlessly. I was hoping my father could find them and fight them but there are so many people working there and a mistake in identification could bring trouble.

I hated to think of that accident when I was so powerless to defend myself. There in the town the boys like to touch girls' breasts to make them grow bigger than normal and it would of course be embarrassing for the girl because people would think that she's played around. Once, also on my way home from cutting grass at school, I walked through the forest on the small hill by our town. I met a man who used to be my brother's friend, but when he got close, he reached out his hand and touched my breast. I had a knife with me for cutting the grass and I threw it at him. I cried on the way home but again I could not do anything. At that time, if someone explored you the feeling was almost like rape. They insult you but who will help? Ugh, the men love that and they will keep doing it.

My younger sister Yayang recently told me that she was raped when she was about fifteen. They were having a party after school. One of her girlfriends asked her to come to a room, and then locked the door from the outside. She tried to get out; she was screaming but the music was very loud and the boy inside did not even stop. He forced my sister. She begged and cried but the boy raped her and destroyed her virginity. She went home broken-hearted and pale. I remember the day she came home. She was so pale and sad but did not say anything. So the accident passed for many years without anyone knowing.

I was upset to learn that I got through all the hard and painful time but hers was even worse. She kept the secret to herself for many years. She never told anybody except my sister Ita and me, finally. I asked her why she did not tell us before and she said "How could I? I was just fifteen and nobody would help. If they knew they would blame me for going to the party."

I thought she was right. My sister was the one who had a smooth youth and she used to be the one in the family who got all the attention and the most love from my parents. So she had to carry all her nightmare alone. It was unbearable for her.

Even in my village, when I was around seven years old, I went with some of my friends to bathe by the river. Bathing naked was common in our village and therefore I felt no embarrassment. So we took off all our clothes and went swimming in the cold river. When we came out of the water we rushed to the riverside and put our clothes on in the woods. One of the men who was taking a bath in the same place followed me and as I was standing naked in front of him and shyly covered myself with my clothes, he came closer. He was big smiling and said "Hey you, can we do it?"

I looked at him and I understood his words because I'd heard them many times. As a child I knew the word he used; "it" meant doing something like the dogs do in the street. We saw that and some older boys explained to us what the dogs were doing when their tails were sticking to each other. I put my clothes on quickly and ran after my friends. He luckily did not stop me. I still remember his big smile and how he touched his thing under his worn shorts. He was my neighbour and he was married with some small kids. In the village I was the one who had clean skin and no problem with skin diseases. My skin under my clothes was soft and light and my friends were sometimes jealous as their skin was dark and dirty with scars here and there. They had to help their parents in the plantation and were in the sun all the time.

17

What a Life!

M Y PARENTS' HOUSE stands near the river, almost on it. It's made of wood, seven-by-nine metres, and at the rear it has a temporary building for a kitchen and the walled open space where my father works, killing and cutting up his pigs. He raises local pigs and sometimes proudly raises huge white Balinese pigs on his small piece of land across the river. Every afternoon, he paddles his dugout canoe across the heavy current to bring the pigs food and every week or two, he goes to Christian houses and Chinese houses around town to collect orders for pork. After he's sure he has enough orders, he brings the pig in a bamboo basket from his small pens to the house, where he fills an empty oil container with a lot of water and drowns the pig in it. When the struggling pig is half dead, he stabs its neck with a long sharp knife and collects the blood in a basin. (The blood is to cook the intestine.) He has to to do it this way to reduce any objections since we live among Muslim people and Papah doesn't want them to know that he slaughters pigs in the house. Sometimes when a pig screams, Papah orders Mamah to turn on the tape recorder as loud as she can before pushing the pig in the water.

Usually I take Karina away when Papah is killing but sometimes she slips out to the kitchen and stands behind the doors to satisfy her curiosity. Then she runs back and jumps in my lap. After the preparations, Papah loads the pork on his old motorbike and goes around town, coming back by late afternoon with a handful of money. Our Muslim neighbours used to frown at Papah when he passed their houses along the alley where we live but he got tired of that and purposely carried the pork wrapped only in a plastic bag with blood dripping all the way; when they stopped wrinkling their faces, he again wrapped his meat carefully.

Karina sometimes comes home grumbling and complaining with her child voice, and reports to me that neighbourhood children call her Pork Eater and don't want to play with her. People eating pork are dirty, that's what the parents say. But she says, "Karina has friends in school, so no matter, ya?"

When I started my job as a guide, I was required to go to the forest all the time. When my neigbours knew, they started talking behind my back and called me a prostitute. They said I screwed with the guests and that's how I made money. Made dollars. They put jealous eyes on me. And they started to stay away, saying that I bring the contagious AIDS from the guests. What people in my town think is that the sickness came from the tourists and they should be kept away. Tourists are dirty. They eat pork, and so do I. So I was to be avoided, like them. I tried not to care and I kept going to the forest. My parents told me not to listen to all those words. "They never give you money so why do you care?" they told me.

The first time I joined Pak Thomas to take guests to the park, I was so nervous. I'd seen foreigners a couple of times before during the high seasons in my town. They stayed at the Blue Kecubung hotel close to our school. I would climb the three-metre-high wall of my school yard and, when we saw tourists passing, I'd jump over just to greet and talk to them for a few minutes. We called anyone foreign "the lost tourist" because there was nothing to see in our town. But ever since the wall-jumping program my interest in them grew and I also saw the Great Apes Conference held near the national park, where I joined the Dayak dance welcoming group. There I saw a lot of foreigners and I really wished that I could speak good English so that I could communicate with them.

When our dance tutor told us that Jane Goodall was coming to the conference, I was curious to know who this was. I was thinking that he mentioned "John Goedal" and during the dance my eyes were wondering if I could recognize this man.

There in the same place I saw Mrs. Birute Galdikas walking briskly surrounded by her daughter Jane and her Dayak husband Pak Bohap, who looked small and nervous walking beside her. He was once a farmer, a hunter and a woodcutter, but he now lives with Birute in the village of Pasir Panjang close to Pangkalan Bun. She owns a nice big house where there are many Dayak workers. Although many people in our town have never seen her, when I became a guide, I used to see her a lot, especially if she stayed in the park. Tanjung Puting had been a nature reserve since 1939 and was established as a national park in 1986. For years, the PHPA, our government ministry for nature wildlife and protection, has tried to enforce all the laws against ownership of protected animals.

The park, which covers more than 300,000 hectares, has recently expanded, and is home for thousands of orang utans both captive and wild, along with hundreds of other rare animals such as honey bear, clouded leopard, sambar deer and many kinds of rare birds such as king fishers, paradise bird and the holy Dayak bird, hornbill.

When I took guests out to the jungle, my heart was light. It made me happy to tell them about the jungle, the trees, the animals they had never seen before in their lives. During my days in Tanjung Puting, I met Birute numerous times. She sometimes stared at me and went away. To her dining hall or to her cabin. I almost never had a private conversation with her. Once I was there with a group and Birute was there with a crew of film-makers. She talked for many hours in the dining hall and the film-makers kept filming her. They changed the tape a couple of times. The group was deeply impressed.

Once I took an American, a very kind man. He loves the jungle and hiking so we went out often and watched the wildlife. Often we saw orang utans feeding themselves from the trees, moving very slowly from branch to branch. The babies are much like humans. They cry when their friends disturb them and keep their distance from the older ones. My new friend loved to hike so one morning we went to the second station. We prepared our backpacks and made sure we had water. I put my Swiss knife in my pocket. We left our small boat and went into the camp. We went to the ranger's post and showed our permits.

The second station was still very new then. Before, the rangers had used Tanjung Harapan, the first station, as a nursery for the orang utans. It's about an hour downriver by boat and the babies were mostly kept there. But since the place was too close to the village of Tanjung Harapan across from the park, and also the Rimba Lodge, the babies got too used to seeing humans and hardly went to the forest. This is not good as the orang utans should live in the trees. Their real home. So the park authorities decided to open a new station upriver specializing in training the babies to be wild and introducing them to the real forest.

They started with some babies that were taken from people in the town who kept them as pets. They let them sleep outside in the nearby trees. Then at 8 a.m., the rangers woke the babies by calling their names. They tumbled over and over rushing down from the trees to get sweet bananas for breakfast and instant milk with sugar. After they finished the rangers forced the babies to go back to the trees because if they stayed on the ground a wild pig could kill and eat them. It had already happened several times. Baby orang utans are slow movers on the ground so it's difficult for them to escape. The rangers had to be watchful. They would often go back to the woods to make sure the babies were safe. If they found them rolling and playing on the ground, they had to force them back into the trees.

One of the rangers I know quite well is Allan. He comes from Kumai town and works in the first station where there are still five or six babies. Most of them were very sick when they arrived; they suffered from malnutrition, worms, pneumonia or even skin diseases. Allan said it was sad to see the babies like this and there was never enough medicine because it is very expensive. One of his endearing babies was Buntung, a female who was an amputee. She was fat and healthy but quite one-armed. She didn't like to be with the other babies as they bothered her. She moved very slowly and she had difficulty climbing but she always tried even when she fell down.

Now Buntung is wild. She's one of the ones who successfully went back to the forest. But her big friend Gistok has not become independent even though he is almost eight and very healthy. He is the portrait of the naughty, spoiled kid in the camp.

Most of his friends are now living in the forest and Gistok is left far behind. He is too scared to be alone because he lived too long with humans. Allan told me he sometimes takes Gistok to the forest and leaves him but Gistok always sneaks back. Before Buntung and the other babies became wild, they liked to build a nest in the trees by the camp and Gistok always watched them. When the nest was finished and they were ready for sleep, Gistok came and took over the nest. The little ones tried to defend their nest but Gistok was too big for them.

I read in a book that orang utan babies stay with the mother until at least eight years of age. But the babies in the park never had that chance as hunters kill the mothers right in front of their eyes. They do that to capture the baby, otherwise the mother will never release it and is willing to fight to the death. In our town there are many people with pet orang utans. Even though the government forbids it, people still fall in love with them and quietly keep them as pets. The richest businessman in our town who owns a big timber company owns an orang utan as his pet, but no one dares to touch him. Orang utans are good business. People in our town say they sell for a hundred thousand rupiahs. They bring the babies by speedboat to the big foreign ships which sometimes throw their anchors by the mouth of the river in the open sea to load wood. If they sell to a foreigner the price is twice as high.

My grandparents had an orang utan as their pet. They tied him outside by the kitchen. He was around eight to ten years old. They loved Untat very much because he was very funny and helpful. Mamah used to tell us that Untat was already there in 1964 when she arrived, the same year my brother Uber was born. She didn't really like Untat at first because he would escape and explore the kitchen for food. He would clean up all the food in the cooking pan without making a mess at all. The pans would be empty. Sometimes when he escaped, he would go to the neighbour's house if the family had all gone to their *ladang*. He would sneak over and open the areca woven floor neatly so he could climb in. Then he stole *tuak*, the rice wine, and got himself drunk. Back home he walked swaying dreamily. But nobody could get angry with him because he was so funny.

My grandma liked to ask for his help opening coconuts. She would hand him a coconut when she wanted to open it for milk or oil. He would clean the husk and shell with his teeth, but grandma sat next to him and watched to make sure he did not make a hole in the eyes of the coconut and drink the water. He would get diarrhea if they let him drink it. When he finished opening the coconut, she would fight with him because he wouldn't want to give it back. Grandma would pretend to whip him with rattan so he would give the coconut to her. She used to clean her teeth with coconut ash. She would choose the inner ash and bring it down to Topin Dadap where we used to bathe. She did not eat betel leaves like most of the people in our village do. Mamah didn't either. She said it was not nice to have a dark red mouth from that stuff. So they had nice white teeth while most people had dark, black teeth and seldom cleaned them.

My mamah told us that when Untat got diarrhea, they released him so he could go to the jungle and cure himself with certain food or leaves and he would be back a couple of days later with his diarrhea gone. Sometimes the family would release him and let him join them when they visited a neighbour. Then Untat would sit down and make himself some betel nut. He would watch how the people did it and take a piece of the betel leaf and mix the lime, fold it nicely and eat it. His lips and mouth would be red and he would look funny like that. But one day Untat got very bad diarrhea so they had to go to Pangkalan Bun for treatment. They paddled down with him in a boat, but the journey was too long and hard for Untat and he died just as they arrived in the town. That was in 1966.

I don't know what they did with Untat's body.

My papah used to tell us that he and his friends in the village once went hunting and one of his friends killed a huge orang utan. He said he was different from an orang utan, more like a human. He had very long hair and it was light yellow in colour and he walked straight. He was sure it was not an orang utan. He said it was *tambalui*, the creature who is almost half god because he is so old and holy. His friend almost could not carry the body. He said it had a human face.

Time in the forest is the happiest time for me. I love to come up the river by boat and inhale the morning air. Fresh, no pollution, and cool. Once I was with a professor who loved birds a lot. He came from the UK but he was living in New Zealand. There was also a lady with us who was around eighty years old and loved birds as well. She was also from the UK. They were both using the Kalpataru travel agency and I was a freelance guide. I took them on a river boat and spent almost ten days in the national park. I loved being with them and they taught me a lot about birds. Every morning we set our program by cruising the river and taking our breakfast on the water. We had our breakfast on the boat while watching birds and every time we saw birds, we stopped the boat and they would take pictures. Ruth, the old lady, was always taking pictures of birds, proboscis monkeys and sometimes orang utan we found by the river. They taught me a lot about how to identify bird sounds and to recognize them when they fly by the movement of their body and the style of flying. There are about five kinds of hornbill we have in the national park. The most common is pied hornbill with black and white feathers. And black hornbill with almost completely black feathers. With those guests I passed an exciting time. In the morning we would do what we called "bird hunting," and by the mid-morning we would be cruising up to the main station. This camp was named after the famous Louis Leakey. And this station is also where Mrs. Birute Galdikas started her career studying orang utans.

Birute, she is really famous outside, but not many people here have ever seen her, as I said.

To make the clinic for orang utans in her place, she's been granted a big amount of money by the Orang utan Foundation International. She's the president. It makes me wonder why, since we have a new clinic with a dedicated veterinarian in the first station of the park. What they need is some equipment and medicines for the orang utans who are threatened by many diseases: TB, skin diseases, worm diseases, diarrhea and bad flu. Some of the babies have died from disease. The park is struggling to save them but they run out of medicines and there is not enough money for equipment.

The park ranger, Allan, has told me how he feels when all he has to feed the babies are unripe bananas. He willingly boils the unripe bananas first, so they will be able to digest them. Elsewhere, some big orang utans outside Birute's kitchen in Camp Leakey enjoy rice and sweet apples.

I talked once with the former head of the park who was arguing many times with Birute because he did not agree with feeding the orang utans human food. It's the reason big males like Kosasih, Bagong, Emeng, Tom, Uranus and some others keep coming back. Those orang utans were all confiscated and used to live among humans, but now they are huge and dangerous. For years they were under Birute's supervision at Camp Leakey. But now, because of her policies, she has lost her permit.

Anyone who ever visited Tanjung Puting National Park probably knows Kosasih. He's the orang utan leader in Camp Leakey. He has lots of girlfriends around camp but his closest girlfriend is Siswi who had a baby named Selamat (Survive). Siswi is a very jealous young lady who attacks her rivals face to face and thinks Kosasih is only hers. But sometimes when she isn't hungry she can be very sweet. The boatmen sometimes give her some soap paste and she loves to play with it, putting it in the water, rubbing it on her arm and creating foam, then licking it. Orang utans have a food which tastes similar to this soap. Sometimes the boys also give her a piece of cloth and she will pretend to wash it just like the boatmen do when they do their laundry. Normally when our boat arrives, Siswi and Selamat are already on the dock waiting for us. It's fun to see the mama washing with the baby hanging on her breast.

Before she lost her license to work with orang utans, Birute's face was smooth and calm, her voice was very soft, talking Indonesian with a funny accent to her all-Dayak staff. I sometimes wondered how she managed to go to the forest with such a heavy body. "She was always in camp" said one of her staff, a friend of mine. He told me that Birute never went to the forest to "follow" orang utans. Her staff did that for her and collected all the reports. In the dawn, some boys were already awake and preparing the equipment: knife, notebook, binoculars, package of lunch and a hammock. "We are not allowed to go back until the orang utan we follow sets up a nest to sleep in the evening," my friend continued. He said that they go deep into the forest looking for a wild orang utan and if they find one, they have to follow him, noting all the movements in their notebook and what tree he forages in. It takes a whole day until he makes his nest. Then the boy notes the place and comes back the next morning to the same place before the orang utan wakes up so he won't lose him. He starts to follow him again and again for whole days, making notes to deliver to Birute in the evenings. The "follow" sometimes takes a week or so before they lose him.

But once I took a guest trekking in the forest and we saw a boy lying in a hammock between two small trees. He got up when he saw us and said, "I lost the orang utan I've been following."

"Then how will you make a report to Birute?" I asked him.

He shrugged, went back to his hammock and waited there till evening before he walked back to the camp and delivered his incredible report. My friend told me that the work was hard and the payment was little. "Sometimes we get bored and write whatever we want so we can have something to report," he said.

"Does Birute ever find out?"

"I do not think she cares," replied my friend.

Birute was probably busy then, typing all the reports and claiming them as her own. "I think you are the one who should be called 'professor,' not her," I laughed at him. "You are the people of the forest and you know much more than Birute knows about it, but you do not have any degree and you are only a little people, that's the problem." I finished the chat, waved to Birute's other staff by the dining hall and slipped away to join my guest who was tailing some baby orang utans along the trail out of camp.

Maybe the camp was named after Birute's late mentor Louis Leakey to respect him, but nobody seems to care about it now.

"Birute makes our work difficult," the rangers complain. When she was still working there, they had to struggle over her decision not to obey the regulation and keep feeding the orang utans food that was not good for them. The result was enormous. The orangs kept staying in the camp.

Even now, her organization is selling tours. Pak Herry, a massive, friendly and warm smiling middle-aged man, and head of the park, once frowned over my guest's questions about this. "Birute is powerful and the world believes blindly in her," he said with his soft, well-spoken English.

I keep thinking about his words. I know where Birute lives. I've seen Dayak women and girls there, doing cleaning and cooking. Some of them carried some baby orang utans past us to the back of the house when I was there. I've seen two of those girls carrying tiny baby orang utans in diapers. I asked one of them where the babies sleep at night. "Just around here, in the trees" She pointed up. Some women were busy at the firestove outside the main house cooking and some boys walked to and fro. At that time I was bringing a baby orang utan that had just been taken from its owner. An old friend named Ali, who was working for Birute, came by my house trying to rent a canoe. I asked where he was going and he said he was on the way to confiscate a six-month-old baby orang utan across the river. So I joined him. When we arrived at the village named Kampung Raja Seberang, my friend Ali told the orang utan owner that he wanted to take the baby. He took out his camera and took the baby's picture.

The man did not say anything. I noticed that one of the baby's fingers was cut off. He said it was cut off by accident when his little daughter was playing with the baby orang utan. That's why they called him Si Puntung, Stubby. When Ali reached over for the baby, the owner started to protest, but Ali said he was from the Orang utan Foundation and it was forbidden to have an orang utan as a pet.

The owner was angry and hurt and thought a man in the village — another friend of mine named Ujang — had reported him to the Orang utan Foundation. He said if Birute had asked him to give the baby away he would have done it willingly — he was an old friend of Birute's husband, Bohap — but he didn't want someone coming to his house and taking the baby without any explanation. He was very angry and said he wasn't a thief. They should ask him politely and not just show their power.

That's how I ended up in her house. I went to the back where the girls were holding baby orang utans and we gave Si Puntung to one of them. That was two years ago and I don't know what happened to him after that. He's not at Tanjung Puting. He's probably growing up in Birute's house where he will never know the jungle or meet with his relatives. He's probaby enjoying rice and sweet apples. What a life! But there is not much forest around. The main road is only 10 metres away and we could hear the cars roaring past when I was there and my thoughts wandered to the baby orang utans in the park, to the small white painted clinic in Tanjung Harapan, sometimes full of sick baby orang utans and the PHPA struggling to help them. I wonder why the world laid its hope on Birute to help the orang utans here in Kalimantan. Those poor orang utans suffer from diseases without enough medicine while Birute is zooming by in her nice boat along with numerous tourists telling the world with her soft motherly voice that she feels sorry for all that death in the park and blaming the PHPA.

18

Travelling

I HAD DECIDED TO GO to Bali to study German and Japanese, which would help my work, so I worked very hard and spent most of my days taking guests to the forest. The journey usually took a few days in Tanjung Puting or the Dayak villages. Once I spent ten days taking a Swiss couple to a Dayak village and I missed my daughter a lot. But I had to go. I had to earn more money so I could go to Bali and take Japanese or German courses for at least three months.

For two weeks I was with the Swiss couple and we went up to Sekombulan at the head of Delang River. I'd met them in the airport and learned that they wanted to see Pastor Stanis so I helped them and took them to the pastoral compound and took care of their permit. I became their guide.

The Dayak where I was born did not know that the government actually gave them a name to identify them, the

Ngaju. Most of us just like to be Dayak Delang, after the name of the river. They have a strong accent with deep and pressing words. Their adat (traditional law) was different from Dayak Ngaju adat even though there was some similarity here and there. When I lived there, we came down to town by the river using a seven-to-ten-metre longboat which had an engine. It took at least two or three days to get down because we had to pass so many rapids.

But now we have the new road which connects the village to the other villages and twice a week we have a small public bus which comes up. In the dry season the journey is not bad, but in the rainy season the journey is difficult and dangerous and there is no guarantee that you will reach the village in one day. Often you have to spend the night on the road because the bus is stuck and stranded. Most of the time the bus is full. If it's coming up from town the passengers will have sugar, salt, onions or kitchen wares or even rice because there are some villages which suffer from starving. If the bus is coming down from the village, it will be full of vegetables, chickens, pigs and passengers. Nowadays, many villagers who owned boats are selling them because of the advantages of going down by bus. It's faster and cheaper. Now from Kudangan (the last stopping place) many young people like to go down to town.

When I visited the village with the Swiss couple we stayed for a week in Sekombulan, where my uncle got killed. First we stopped in Kudangan after eight hours of long journey and I saw that the village was still the same and many of the familiar faces appeared. That night when everybody slept, my aunty told me that the Kudangan villagers had been fighting over my grandparents' land. A couple named Untai and Anti and another couple, Una and Ulo, claimed that the land was theirs. My uncle had been fighting to hold the land because my grandfather legally got the land from the chief of law because he was a respected teacher. Wanting him to settle there, they gave him a big piece of land. My uncle and my father, who had been there recently, showed the paper to the chief, to the army, which was taking part in the case, and to the police as well. They could not see any mistakes in it. It was all legal. But Untai and Anti cultivated a piece of rice field on my grandpa's land and then sold it to a neighbour for 500,000 rupiahs.

When my uncle found out, the neighbour who bought the land got embarrassed and did not confess. So he lost the money he'd spent and now he was asking for it back from Untai and Anti. They apparently lost the case, but it looked like they did not want to give up so they threatened my uncle. They said, "Your brother Ian is already killed, another will get his turn as well."

Those neighbours were jealous because our family came from a different tribe, different area and now owned such a big ladang in the village.

I was travelling in a truck with the Swiss couple and the next morning we went on up to Sekombulan. We let the people who wanted to join us ride in the open back of the truck. I told my friends the story of my uncle who was killed. There was a chief in the old village of Sekombulan who was an orator, always making speeches, very persuasive. Our government wanted to change this chief and replace him with my uncle Ian. But the former chief didn't want to give up. He was mad and he thought it was better to be a chief than not to be a chief. That way he had more chances to get some money. We have some contributions from our government. Mostly we must give the money to the people who need it — it's kind of credit — and then they will pay it back. But that chief always kept the money for himself and the people got nothing.

When the people knew that my uncle was chosen by the government they were excited and made a rice wine party to honour him. Lots of people came and shared the party. One of them handed my uncle a cup of wine in the cup that can be handled only by special persons. Everyone knew my uncle and the former chief were against each other. The old chief even asked some young boys to fight with my uncle's children to scare them. The village was divided in two — but they had made this celebration for my uncle and they had brought the special cup.

A couple of hours after my uncle was served, he felt something wrong in his stomach. He felt pain there and his throat was swollen and he couldn't take anything to eat. His wife tried to feed him a little water from a spoon but he couldn't swallow anything and three days later he died. Before he died he began rolling on the floor. He couldn't hold the pain. My father got the news from a friend, who came to our house in town, but he didn't want to believe what he heard. He had to see for himself. So he went up to the village and got information that the former chief had asked somebody to poison the rice wine because he was jealous. Yes. This was in Sekombulan village. The former chief had poisoned my uncle because he didn't want to give over his position. So he gave poison to my uncle in the rice wine and it killed him.

Nobody investigated.

Dayak people are very good at making poison. One of the materials is from the ipuh tree. We tap the sap and put it on the tip of a dart and use it in a blowpipe. It kills animals in five minutes. We can put a little bit on a dart and shoot an animal and paralyze it. You can catch it after that. Or we can put more on the dart to kill people. It can kill within five minutes. The Dutch were very afraid of this poison. It is really strong.

Some of our villages can also make a poison to catch fish in the big river. Lots of people from other villages will come as well. They collect bark from the tubo tree and then pound it down. They fill the canoe with that because they want to catch big fish, then some people come up to the head water and pour one canoe of tubo poison in the river. The poison drugs the fish. Big and small they will get drunk and float to the surface and the people waiting down river will catch them by hand only. They will catch as many as they can, sometimes up to one canoe full.

Our poison is very dangerous. Even for people.

When we left to go back to town, the back of the truck was full of old and young people carrying chickens and pigs. Suddenly a woman ran up to tell us she was worried that maybe on the way a girl would stop the truck. The girl was running away from the village and hiding somewhere in the forest. She wanted to go to the town but her parents would not allow it. So she ran away hoping to join us on the way. The lady asked us, if we met a girl, just do not pick her up. So we left with the back of the truck full of people, but nobody tried to stop us.

After a couple of months of hard work I thought I had money enough to support me for some months and I decided to go to Bali. I was happy when I was given money from the Swiss couple who had been my guests. They sent it to me because they were pleased that I wanted to study.

When I finished all my preparation, I departed Kalimantan and left poor Karina behind. It was heartbreaking to leave her but I had to do it for our future. I knew that she would miss me but I could not take her with me because my situation was going to be very rough.

19

He Gave Me Nice
Words

I LEFT KALIMANTAN IN March, 1996, and took a second-class Bukit Raya passenger ship.

I tried not to stay in the cabin and to go around from one deck to another, visiting restrooms so I would not get seasick. The waves were quite big, over three metres. After eighteen hours on the ship I arrived in Semarang harbour on central Java. I took a taxi to Purboyo Station where a ticket scalper charged me 20,000 rupiah to go to Jakarta. He said I would get an air-conditioned bus direct to Jakarta. Of course I found out that the bus stopped in Tegal station, where I had to get another bus.

It had no air-conditioning. And the driver kept taking people off the street. It was crowded and hot, but I was lucky to get to Jakarta on the same day, since I had promised my ex-guest who lived there that I would arrive on March 19.

Although it was late at night, Pulogadung Terminal was crowded with people and buses. I went to the phone service a hundred metres from the station carrying my big backpack and finally got my friend on the phone. He said I should come to his house right away and he would have dinner waiting. So I got a taxi. The driver said he knew very well the street that I was looking for so I paid him 15,000 to go direct to the street and asked him not to take me round and round. But we could not find the street because he did not know the area and we spent more than an hour looking.

My friend Benoit is a Frenchman, young, soft spoken and working in a big advertisement company. He lived along with his two maids in a very big house with a garden and swimming pool. I got a big room for myself and he welcomed me with a big pizza. It was good but I couldn't eat much because the taste was still strange on my tongue. I felt very grateful. He had just arrived from Surabaya an hour before I arrived at the bus station and he was also tired.

In the morning we met again and talked for a few minutes before he left to catch a flight to Thailand for four days. I was disappointed because I hadn't a chance to talk longer with him, but he asked his friend Berthrand (another of my ex-guests) to take care of me while he was away.

For four days Berthrand took me to so many places in Jakarta. I knew very well that he was busy with his job, but he always tried to save time for me.

On the last day he took me to the biggest new hotel —

the Sangrilla Hotel in Jakarta, taking me to the bar because I had told him that I wanted to know what a bar looked like. And we had fettucine for dinner there. I felt out of place in the bar with my plain clothes. All the women looked fancy. The fettucine was terrible! Just white pasta with no taste. But I still had a nice time with my friend. After dinner I went back home and waited for the owner of the house. When he came in at 11 p.m., I was so happy to see him that I hugged him. He offered me a kind of drink that tastes light and sweet. Then we said goodnight to each other.

The next day I was in a taxi heading for the train station which would take me to Surabaya. The train was good and quite clean. We stopped in every station on the way to take new passengers. Every time we stopped, lots of young boys and old women carrying baskets tried to sell us many kinds of food, fruit or cigarettes. The journey took a day and a night and I had to take sitting naps in a chair.

In the morning, still dark, we arrived in the Surabaya train station and I headed directly to the bus station by bemo and got a morning bus to Bali.

I spent five days in Ubud trying to collect information about courses, but they only had a Japanese course so I had to take a bus to Sanur to find a German course. When I arrived in Sanur I got the only course available. And I got a room to stay in right away just behind the language building for 50,000 rupiah/month. A Balinese family lived next door.

I didn't make a lot of friends, but Bali seemed to be a nice place. When I visited the beach at Kuta, a man from Kalimantan offered me work as a snake dancer. He had some big pythons. I tried to hold the snakes but they were so scary and slippery that I said, "No snake dancing at all. Not for me."

I took the German course in Sanur for one month, but the tutor sometimes showed up and sometimes not and I got bored, so one day I went to the beach and on the way, I was attracted by somebody playing guitar in the small café by the road. I stopped and had a look. "Hello, How are you? Please come in." I heard a friendly voice greeting me. She was a mid-forties lady who wore heavy make-up and sexy clothes and I greeted her back. This lady named Indah was my neighbour and lived a couple of houses away.

One day I visited her and was surprised to see three little girls by her house. The first girl was about eleven years old and I supposed that she had Japanese blood in her. The second and the last were European mixed-up babies. Their father was Australian. I asked Indah where the father is now and she said that their father went back to his country two years ago and had not been back since.

I did not ask more as she did not want to talk about it. I found out mostly from her children who told me everything even though I did not ask. They said their daddy was sleeping with their babysitter in the same bed. Indah was furious. They had a big fight. She left her husband and ran away to Sulawesi for three months leaving her little girls behind. But finally she decided to go back to her husband who asked her to accept his apology. She accepted but her feeling was already cold; her husband had betrayed her. So, using all the money from the two big jewellery shops they had, she spent crazily for drink and night life and then ended up losing hundreds of millions to a new boyfriend who ran away with the last of the money to Europe. Then it was her husband's turn to be furious and leave his wife behind.

I spent a month in Sanur. I took courses two times a week and I made friends with this lady who I called Mbak Indah (sister Indah). She was not really pretty but she had big breasts, a small waist and big bottom. Many men like her and success always follows her. Once I was curious to know why many young men like to be around her and she said that she wore an amulet in her breast, a diamond stone as small as sand inserted by a medicine man. Every man who sees her breast is caught and falls in love with her. I know this practice still exists with a lot of our women but the people who wear these things are against God because they are using the power of darkness. The power of black magic. The medicine man can put the jewellery in a woman's part such as her bottom or breast or even her secret part. The prostitutes often insert it in their vagina so the men who sleep with them will never leave and always come after them. The jewellery varies from silver or gold to diamonds. The more expensive the jewellery, the stronger the power is.

Many people believe that if somebody inserts the jewellery next to her eyes, the man who catches her and looks deep into her eyes will fall in love immediately no matter what she looks like.

I know that women who wear the stone in their bodies will face great suffering and punishment from God when they die because they use evil power to make them prettier against God's will. Neither earth nor sky will want to accept their bodies so their soul will be in the air and no one will be able to help them. The soul will be restless. When they die, somebody has to make sure that the stone will be lifted out of the body and this can only be done by the same medicine man who inserted it. After it is lifted out, they have to make a special praying ceremony to clarify the body and wash away all the dirty things on it. Then the soul will be at peace and will not wander around looking for help.

Once my mamah told me that she knew a woman who used this stone which we call *susuk*. This woman was in her mid-forties and could not be called pretty. She was only plain if not ugly. She divorced her husband and married a young school-aged boy who lived with them. The boy was young and handsome and she fell in love with him. People tell the story that the young boy was caught by the power of darkness in her. She wore stones in one part of her face and when she was out in the evening and using her make-up, she changed and became very beautiful. The strange beauty which only men can see. Women could not see the change as the power was only for making men's eyes turn blindly. The boy was more suited to be her son. My mamah told me that you can enjoy the power when you're alive but you have to be responsible when you die and that is the time the punishment will be worked. The darkness asking to be paid back for its help.

We believe there is another invisible world where the invisible power lives. Where all the darkness comes from. I believe that the power has worked for Indah this way. I am young, speak good English and people say that I am cute, but most of the young men were always around Indah.

I did not have a boyfriend, but did have a good friend who I met after a week in Sanur when I made a phone call from a telephone box across the street. He was standing by the pavement and whistled to me. When I finished, he called me and I crossed the street. I greeted him and asked for information about a Japanese course around Sanur. His named turned out to be Agung, the common name for the second caste in Bali. Agung was handsome with curly long hair but unluckily he was too short for a man. I liked him as a friend. He sometimes borrowed his father's car to teach me how to drive. We would spend almost half a night going round and round with the car. He asked me to be his girlfriend but I said that was too fast for me and I did not want to be somebody's girlfriend if I was not sure of my feelings.

After that, Agung met me less and less. Sometimes I would not see him for a couple of weeks. It made me lonely. He always was able to find excuses if I asked him where he was on the weekend when he promised to pick me up but didn't show up. He said his mother was sick and had to be sent to the hospital or his father had been sick or he had to attend a ceremony in his village. So he was always busy. . .

Once he asked me what about changing my religion to be Hindu like him so I could marry him. I did not give an anwer as I thought he was only making a joke. I also never dreamed of changing my religion to be Hindu as I saw that the lives of the women in Bali were very rough. They would act as a housewife and take care of the children, house and, at the same time, have to make money and not just that. Everyday they have to make offerings. If you have money then you can buy the ready-made offerings in the market, but if not, you have to search for the flowers and coconut leaves and make offerings by yourself. The men are the ones who live very relaxed in Bali. Sitting and smoking while chatting with friends or spending time gambling and cock fighting while their wives have to turn their ass tumbling over to make sure everything is in order.

Bali is the place where people are not ready for all the development. In Bali, many people got rich because they had land and they built homestays. They make handicrafts and sell the culture to the tourists. Many people for instance in Ubud are very rich. They have beautiful, expensive houses with all modern facilities; they go out in a Mercedes Benz with their sarong on the road, or proudly chat on their cellular phones while squatted on the bank of a small dirty river behind the house doing . . . toilet. . . !! They can absorb the modern life but still that was too fast for them and they could not change the way they live. They have nice bathrooms but they prefer bathing nakedly in the brownish water by the small canal along the roads. Some of my friends who rented the room next to mine in Ubud were always embarrassed if I used miniskirts to go out, but they would freely bathe naked, showing their round breasts casually. Many boys pretended to come up and down the river just to have a chance to glance and enjoy the view of them. For me it was strange. When I was in the village, a child, I would take off my clothes when I bathed in the river, but not when I was a woman. I wear a sarong and stay covered all the time.

20

Night Girls

WHEN I PUT MY AD in the Bali Advertiser: *Looking for Job,* most of the offers I got were from the expat companies. An expat lady sent me a fax and asked for an interview and I went to Bali Tours in Sanur and they offered me one month training there. The operation manager was a kind man and he was very cheerful. He offered to let me stay in one of the rooms upstairs where an English lady used to stay before. No one from the office downstairs got the chance to stay there, so I was very thankful to him. The room was big and nice with air conditioning and a big bed and dressing table. A bathroom was outside next door.

Bali Tours is one of the biggest travel agents in Bali and one of three agents who can arrange all kinds of meetings in Bali such as conferences. They handle big groups ranging from one hundred to even a thousand people at a time. I was lucky because my boss put me right in the MICE department (meeting, incentive, conference and exhibition) where many people dream of being trained.

A few days after I arrived, we handled a big group of eight hundred people from Prudential Insurance Company. It was a success indeed. In the near future Bali will be a main place for such conferences to be held as the costs are much lower compared to other Asian countries such as Hong Kong, Bangkok, Singapore and Malaysia. I was supposed to be in training for the first month, so I did not really know if it would turn into a job there, but I was working with an English lady, which was great. I learned a lot from her and other people who worked there as well.

Soon I bought an old laptop from a German lady who was moving back to her country. I got it very cheap. I was happy then, typing my stories, sure that I could write more stories faster and easier. So I began to arrange myself again and get ready for all the new things. I was staying at the office in the one vacant room they had. It was exciting! I could learn how to do correspondence on a scale that I had not thought of before. Not that I mean to talk too high, but I had come from a faraway island, challenged to survive, and I'd ended up in places that I never thought of when I left Kalimantan.

I stayed for one more month in the office room as there was no one in the office who could judge me at the moment so I had to extend my training time. I learned a lot there and it made me really happy. My computer skills were getting better and I was convinced that my future was getting bright.

If someday I had to leave Bali Tours then looking for a job would not be so difficult any more.

When two months were over, I rented a small place close to the office with a bed and bathroom in it. The price I got for that room was very cheap. Well, the place where our office was located is also the place where most of the prostitutes live. Those girls rent the rooms of Javanese or Balinese owners and go out when somebody calls and needs their services. The place where I stayed had no night girls so I felt good about that but it was difficult being a lone woman there. People thought if I went out in the night I was looking for foreigners. They advised me that I should not wear shorts when I went out. I was very irritated with that. I said to them that I did not care what people said about me when I went out wearing shorts because I was just going some blocks from my place for dinner in a small restaurant. I know that I am different from those girls and have a good job which supports me to live. I would not go out wearing heavy thick Levis and long arm sleeves in hot sticky Sanur. Forget it. What I think is that they have to accept my style, if not they can mind their own business. So every night I went out to have dinner paddling my push-bike in my shorts. I have many better things to do than worry about what people think. Sometimes I said to friends that the girls here are not as happy as I am. The girls here, they don't even dare to go out with foreigners as people will judge them as night girls. I used to go out to have dinner with a Dutch friend and the girls usually did not want to talk to me as if I had contagious diseases, as if I was a sack of AIDS. I said that I was having fun indeed and they were not. But sometimes my brain wanted to burst when I heard my neighbours, who are mostly young women, giggling and talking about me. I once almost fought a girl who was screaming at me when my foreign friend picked me up to have dinner. Right after we passed, she yelled at us and I asked my friend to stop and I got ready to jump her. My Dutch friend was alerted by my anger and got going even faster. He was annoyed with me and said that I should not hear what the people say because he knows I am not like they think.

21

Just So Different
from Kalimantan

WHEN I WAS WORKING in Bali Tours the manager told me many things about Sai Baba and showed me a video of him. He lived in India and millions of people were praying and coming to him. He could cure sickness, bring happiness, and he knows everything.

It seemed that Sai Baba did all the miraculous things Jesus did. Teaching people about love. He said there is only one religion, that is the religion of love. He came to give us peace and love and to unite us again. My manager Jelantik was eager to tell me many things about him and I was too confused to think. What he said was Sai Baba had lived before and is now reincarnated. Jelantik said he would come a third time after this. He was like Jesus and he does many things like Jesus. The difference is that Jesus lived in the past where no TV or telephone was yet but Sai Baba is now living in the modern world. Many people believe that he is God by what he said and did.

Jelantik showed me the video which showed all his miracles in front of thousands of people coming from all over other countries. He could create everything from his hands and he was giving the ash which was pouring from his palm. He said the ash is where we come from and what we will be after. It kind of resembled human life. Nothing is eternal in this world. This man, Sai Baba, would build schools, houses for poor people, hospitals . . . all free of charge. It's difficult to believe but he was well known to people and many of them believed in him. I don't know how to tell this here. Better I go back to my own story.

All the time in Bali I kept changing jobs and moved to and fro. I wrote to Karina but not regularly. When I got my salary I sent a little to her for her milk and food. Many times I was searching for toys for her because she loves toys and she loves clothes. On my last visit she insisted on using my lipstick and brushed her hair nicely. "Look, she is very pretty, isn't she?" I talked proudly to Lilis one morning when we had a chat. She was much taller and always kept herself neat and clean. Sometimes this surprised me, since she is only seven years old. On my departure, she hugged me and held my legs tightly. I could feel her grieve for me. But I had to go back to Bali. Again I had to leave her.

When I went back to Kalimantan for that visit, I met

with my sisters Lilis and Yayang and my brother Leo. He had stopped his study and now only stayed home and got drunk all the time. My poor mamah. I really wanted to give many things to her but my brother would not let anything come to the house and would sell it right after it arrived. My mamah was dreaming about a quiet life and they could not fulfill anything as long as my brother still lived there. I worried about Karina having to live in the house in which things were always being broken or threatened. I wanted to take her to Bali and be with her all the time.

In Bali everything is just so different from Kalimantan, but I learn things. I am learning how to drive a car, which I couldn't do in Kalimantan. I am learning about the cargo business, about Sai Baba, and about life in a different place.

One time in Bali I went down to the beach at Kuta to see the sunset. There I met my new friend Ferry, a beachboy who came from Sumatra three years ago. He was twenty-five years old. In the daytime, he taught surfing to anybody who asked him. But he complained because his skin turned dark. He said many of his beachboy friends advised him that guests really love dark skin, the darker the better no matter if you already look like the bottom of a cooking pan. And it would help him to get a Western girl friend. He said he didn't like to be dark. "Looks dirty," he said.

I tried to advise him to find another job and live somewhere else. "If you have enough money to pay, then you can get the job you want," he said bitterly. I knew what he meant because if we don't have family or money who can help, we can never dream about getting a job especially in the government. When I was in Kalimantan, I applied for jobs in many places but the first thing they asked is if I have family who work for the government, then they would try to do their best, or if not you have to pay for the job and the amount sometimes does not make sense. Many of the people give antique jars to the key person in the government if they want to have a job. Forget about the paper test because it is only a formality.

One evening I went to Kuta and met Ferry again. It felt good to talk to him because he was kind and we always had good fun when were were on the beach. "There will be many police patrolling here," he said. "We better move before we're arrested for nothing."

We moved to the main road. It was about 11 p.m. and when we walked past the empty market Ferry warned me that we had to be careful because the security were everywhere. "We didn't do anything, how can they arrest us?" I said stubbornly and sat down.

Ferry got nervous and tried to force me to move but suddenly a fat middle-aged policeman came up. "Hey you, just come to the post for a moment," he said coldly.

Ferry got up and I had no idea what was happening. We followed the policeman to the post and he asked us to go in and we sat on two wooden chairs. He then took out his notebook and pen and started interrogating Ferry. He asked for his identity card and asked what was happening between us. Ferry said nothing happened and we were only having a little argument. The policeman wrote all the information down in his notebook. I was annoyed and did not have any idea why he was questioning us.

I never like the police!

One day I promised to meet a friend for the weekend but he did not show up because he joined the campaign of Megawati, the first daughter of Soekarno our first president. I found out that Megawati would speak close to where I worked so I went there with my push-bike and when I arrived a big bunch of people had gathered around the house. I went in and saw her very close. She was a mid-forties lady a little bit fat and supposed to be pretty when she was young. She still looks pretty. She gave a speech in front of hundreds of her followers and meanwhile the cameramen were busy filming her. When I arrived the speech was almost finished. Her people led her to a small yard where a Balinese dancer was performing a funny dance. Everyone was laughing. Finally the performance finished and Ibu Megawati — which her followers always call her — was ready to go. She passed not as far as one metre in front of my nose and people were trying to shake hands with her, but I did not move my hand as I do not think it is necessary. I am not one of her followers. It was just interesting for me to see how people adored her as if they are ready to die for her.

Her followers came by hundreds of motor bikes which followed her car with a deafening noisy sound. I had to be careful because most of her followers are young people and look wild and hot. My mamah would kill me if she found out that I attended this campaign as she is one who voted for

Golongan Karya (Golkar) the main party in Indonesia. My mamah used to tell me not to choose another party except Golkar; otherwise she would get fired. I could not get her explanation as I think that an election is about freedom to choose. I told her the basic principle of our election is LUBER (*langsung, umum bebas dan rahasia*) which means directly, open/public, free and secret. So what I think is that I can choose the party I like. But I still chose the one she chose and for me it does not make any difference.

The place where they held Megawati's speech was in the area of brothel houses, but it seems that the local government closed its eyes to such practical things. Once I went down the road in the evening on my push-bike and I saw a big sign that says Belanjong Street. I thought it might be leading to the beach so I took that turn. What I found was a slim dark road which leads to the brothels. The music, the girls, men all mixed in the night breath. I was terrified and tried to find a way out. Finally I asked a boy by a small stall and he pointed to a dark path on the right side. I drove my push-bike out while some dogs barked at me. So I was tumbling over to drive my bike on the dark bumpy path. What I did not under-stand is why they put the sign there if that is only a way of leading people to the brothels. The road first was asphalt but slowly turned smaller and darker. I once saw a police car go up the small path in front of the Bali Tours building and within a few moments they came out again. No girls in the car. So I tried to find out what they were doing there and the story turned out that the police were asking money from every brothel. What I wonder is where the money goes.

Now, in Bali, I try to build my life again. I go to discotheques. I try to be modern and enjoy the life I have not had in Kalimantan. I am happy and free, but I cannot lie about being lonely. I miss my daughter, but I still do not dare to bring her to Bali as the situation is very rough and I don't know whether my job is steady or whether I'll have to move again and find another one. I think Karina is better with my parents where she has a home and food and love. Sometimes my family can use the phone near their house to call me at work and I'm happy to find out that Karina is healthy. I don't say all the things that I'm thinking about.

I enjoy other places but deep inside I want to be in Kalimantan because it's so wonderful to wake up in the morning surrounded by the forest. First we open our eyes. Everything is green. Butterflies. Birds. Those are such happy times, thinking that you are part of the jungle. I remember how happy I was when I was around my friends, the boatmen and rangers. I always had good treatment from them. They always prepared my bed in the places I really liked and they would put lots of pillows around me and they would joke that the pillows protected me from being raped by one of them. And in the morning just before I woke up they would prepare tea for me. I felt like family with them.

Every time when I'm in the jungle I feel my spirit. The smell of the forest, how fresh the swampy water is when we pass it while watching something in it that maybe we can see — a turtle swimming or a small fish. Another thing that sometimes made me happy was watching the trees and explaining what kind they are.

I remember one day I was with a guest who was not really interested in orang utans or other animals. But he was so excited to do tracking down in the jungle. I remember taking him quite far away from Camp Leakey. We went deep into the forest and found so many things there. I explained those things to him because I knew most of the plants since I come from a small village surrounded by forest. I told him about the kerangas tree — that orang utans love to eat the young leaves but the sap is very dangerous because it contains such high acidity it makes us burn and itch if we touch it. I told him some Dayaks use the sap to cure tumors and boils. They believe it cures skin diseases. My mother told me that we could actually eat the fruit too, but first we must open it carefully without touching the sap. This is the most difficult part. After we peel the fruit we put it in a sack and cover it in running water for a day or two until all the sap runs out. After that only the soft, white meat of the fruit is left. Then we can boil it or fry it. Many people don't want to deal with this fruit because if they get burned, it leaves a long ugly mark like broken skin. I was surprised to see orang utans consume the purplish leaves without getting burned but sometimes we can see black spots on their mouths from eating karangas leaves and rattan fruit.

Rattan fruit has a sweet and bitter taste and is a bit sticky from the sap. Dayak Tumon people used to make *jeronang* from rattan fruit. It's a natural dye for colouring bark cloth. They take the fruit and pound it and extract the water. Then they get the starch and dry it. They use it to colour many kinds of things from bark cloth to weaving.

A year ago one of my mamah's students didn't come home after school in the afternoon. Her family thought maybe she was playing at her friend's house. By morning, her parents were really worried because she still hadn't come. They waited the whole day. Then they asked people to try to find her.

She was in the fifth grade — about nine or ten. And finally they found her very far away. My mamah's school is a little bit outside of town, and surrounded by forest. And they found her there, very scared. She told her parents about her experience. She said she went to the forest — it's not so far — by herself. She said a man followed her. She got scared and kept away from him, but she didn't realize that she was running even further into the forest.

This man followed her and even chased her. She ran and the man chased her and he got her and choked her, she said. But she managed to fight him. She fought and fought, finally released herself, then ran. The man had a knife and he came after her. It was almost dark. She tried to hide herself. She jumped in some water — there's a small stream — and she jumped in and stayed under until the man lost her track. A whole night she stayed in the water. She was found by some people, and a couple of days ago they found out that the man came from a small village we call Kualajelai. He used to come up to find heads. He gets payment from people who need the heads for offering before making a new building.

Now my father is really worried about my little daughter, Karina. He says, "Never leave her alone on the street." He says, "People have found bodies without heads. Babies, children, one or two years old. They kidnap the babies." My father, when he says it, is just very worried about Karina. Most headhunters like to find babies because they can't defend themselves. They give them some candies then ask them to come with them. In the old days the heads had to be a certain size — but not now. Because the motive, it's not for the dying ceremony any more. When they want to build a house or a bridge — for a timber company or something like that — they bury the first pole, the first pillar, and they put the head under it, with a little mantra because when they try to build a bridge without any head or they use a cow head or goat head, it doesn't work. They say the bridge might just float away or get broken up in few months, even though the bridge is really in good shape. So they need a human head to offer.

In spite of this, the knowledge and the experience of the Dayak people should not be lost for ever. I want this to last. And the culture of the forest. I wish that our next generation will know what the Dayak is and how we are, the way we live and how important the forest is for us because we get all the most important things from it. We pick up the wood from the forest for building, furniture, fire wood and many things. We get wild vegetables to eat, wild red mushrooms, fruit, flowers for offerings — all from the forest. We get our medicines from the forest, using all the different parts of the plants from root, bark and sap to the leaves.

From bamboo skin we make *takin*, a big basket or tang-guk, a simple basket to catch fish.

We use rattan to make a back pack called ladung for men. A long time ago, hunters used it to keep heads. Now we use it to carry forest materials.

22

Another Village

SOMETIMES I'D PREFER to live in a place where it's not too crowded; in the country, with lots of trees — with nature around me. With plenty of land where I can grow everything. I always dream about having a small house with a yard around it where I can grow vegetables. I could raise Karina and she could attend school nearby. I remember my childhood, when I was helping my father plant rice or plant vegetables around the house. I remember my father was very happy when he was in our Dayak village. We had more, we had food because my father had a big ladang.

Now Papah is getting old and suffers from a heart ailment and the spirit tries to protect him. Once my papah almost died. In his suffering, he laughed softly and pointed to the door and said that his friend was getting closer and coming to pick him up. My hair was standing up because nobody was at the door. My papah kept an old bottle with liquid in it somewhere, and he asked for that bottle then. My mamah was searching for it with tears in her eyes, thinking that her husband would be passing away soon. But I had removed the little bottle sometime before because I thought it was only a dirty bottle. So nobody could find it. My papah said the bottle was holy and it was taboo to destroy it. It contained little mantras.

My oldest brother Eby is a teacher in a small village outside our town. In the afternoon I really enjoy watching fishes in the small river behind his house. The water is very clear and sweet. Karina also loves to be there as she loves flowers a lot and she searches for wild flowers and collects as many as she can. In my parents' house there are not so many flowers as it stands by the river which frequently floods. When Karina puts flowers behind both ears she comes and says to me, "Mami, do I look like a princess?"

I say, "Oh you look like an angel" and she smiles. She never knew her father and now she's growing faster and prettier as each day passes. Karina got most of her father's features. She's pretty and she's tall and will be taller than I am someday soon.

My heart sinks every time I see the forest being cut down by machines, dragged down the Delang River, the Batang-kawa River, down to the Lamandau River to the huge timber company in Pangkalan Bun.

I'd like to live in the country, yes, with lots of trees . . . but I think if we still lived in the place where I was born, it would be very hard for us, especially for Mamah. My father would never have stopped being a farmer. He would still be hunting wild boar and deer. He would still be tapping the palms, tapping rubber. I think my father would be happier if he could do the same work he had before. So he can feel like a man.

My younger brother Leo might be a little bit better if we lived in the village, because he would have to get up and work very hard. My father wouldn't be able to support him with money. Maybe if he lived there, he would have married early and have his own responsibility. But here, he can go on being wild, doing everything, and always getting money whenever he needs it. Whatever he wants he always gets. In the village, at least he'd have a little responsibility for his life.

But for me, if we hadn't moved down river, I would never have had an education. I think I would maybe be married when I was seventeen. I'd have five kids by now. Even more, maybe. I'd be helping my husband with the farming. The women in my village, they're hard workers, collecting fire-wood and finding the vegetables in the forest. Maybe a girl there is happy like that because she thinks she has everything that she needs. She thinks it's enough.

I could do it. And maybe I would be happier than I am now. But maybe not. Maybe I would be an unlucky woman with a big bunch of children and lots of hard work and never know about life outside the village. I think now that I'm lucky because I can find out about another village, how its life is. Not just in the one place, stuck there.

My older sister went back to Kudangan to teach for six months. Our government made a rule that if somebody wants to be a teacher, they must teach in their own village for at least six months, sometimes more — one or two years — before moving to another place. Otherwise some people don't like to move back to their own village. My sister went out there with her six-month-old son while her husband was teaching in Palangkaraya. But now people say to live in such a place is very difficult because lots of people come and there's competition everywhere. There are many more people but mostly they are government employees or teachers. They don't own land, they don't own a garden or ladang. So what we have is not enough to feed all the people there. Sometimes they don't buy a thing. They keep asking, asking. "Well, they eat!" as Mamah always says. "You know a woman comes to the house and asks for vegetables. She wants the pumpkin and she keeps asking and asking. If she wants to, she just goes over to the garden because she's heard about my nice garden with lots of vegetables."

Now, young people mostly leave the village, and just children and old people stay and work the ladangs. Because they don't have enough young people who help them, the ladangs aren't big and sometimes they have problems because their rice is not enough to last until the next harvest. And they get poorer and poorer because, if they have some money, they must buy rice for themselves. Everything gets worse.

Eventually, they sell their property just to keep alive. When they have something — antique jars from their family, something they got from a great-grandfather or another generation — they sell it. Now not too many people have those things and they are even more expensive because there aren't so many any more.

The last time I visited Kudangan was with my Canadian friend. She wanted to visit my village, so I went up with her.

There was a burial ceremony for one of the old, respected families. There was only a praying, no bagondang party, no dancing because since Christianity came, only a few people, old people, have their own old faith.

I'd met Linda in 1995 when I was still working with Best Tours. I'd met her in the airport with her two beautiful daughters, young and very confident. And I'd joined them as their guide to the nature reserve. On her second trip, when Linda came alone to work on her book *The Follow*, I was there again and accompanied her and she encouraged me to write about my culture, my life as a Dayak woman — a tribe of people who are known as uneducated people from the hinterland. There I started a new section of my life.

On her third trip, she wanted to see my village, so I flew from Bali to Jakarta and to Kalimantan to my hometown, Pangkalan Bun. When we wanted to take Karina to Kudangan, my father joined us because he did not want to let Karina go without him.

The journey my little girl experienced was much different from mine a long time ago. Only five years ago we had to make preparation for a long journey by river on a small ten-metre boat with a single engine or even on a row boat, taking as many supplies as possible and preparing to stay on the boat for many days or even weeks. There would be a smooth journey or a rough journey depending on the river's mood. It might be suddenly angry, rushing fast, violent flood water from the head of the river crushing everything on its way, drowning and hiding the sharp rocks under its surface, hitting and crushing the helpless boats above.

Now we can leave the village by the red soil timber road. It takes almost a whole day, but as soon as we got the road down to Benuo, the river town, people in the village sold or even abandoned their boats and preferred to go down to the town by road, which was faster and cheaper. The lovely trip by longboat passing the green of the woods, the white rapids and looking down through the clear water of the river is no longer done any more. It's even hard to find someone in the village who still owns a boat.

The journey to Batangkawa River along the left branch and the Sungai Buluh River passing Belantikan River along the right branch is still done but mostly by river transport and they no longer travel up the Delang. In May 1997, when I went back to the village with my friend and my father and Karina, we took the timber road and they were building a huge bridge connecting one side of the Lamandau River to the other, where the road was split by the water. The bridge was unfinished so we put the rented car on the old ferry but overhead we could see what was to come. Soon it will be done and there will be no more emergency ferry crossing the river, carrying vehicles on its floating belly; all the traffic coming up and the down from the once remote Dayak area will be as usual as a daily need.

A big business is in cutting down trees. Before, if they cut wood around our village, it would have been very difficult to sell because we were very far away from the timber company. (We had a timber company called Ptalas on the border of West Kalimantan.) Now lots of young girls, young people, work in that company. They get their salary every month. Not like before. Before they just helped in the ladang and they got nothing, except for rice; they'd keep it in their rice barn and it was just enough to feed their family for one year until the next harvest. If they sold some of the rice, they would not have enough to feed themselves until the next harvest, so they never had cash.

Once my friend told me that her brother-in-law brought down wood on the Delang River, rafting it. They had a thousand pieces. It was a long journey and when they passed the river of Topin Bini a dangerous rapid was waiting. They tied one boat in front of the log raft to pull and one in the back to keep balance and arranged the wood in order.

When they started slowly taking the raft through the rocky, fast rapids a policeman came and pointed his gun in the air and shouted to them to stop. Her brother-in-law of course couldn't stop when they were right in front of the dangerous rapids, so the only thing they could do was keep going in order that the boat would survive the rocks and fast-moving water. But the policeman was still pointing his gun and when he saw they kept going, he pointed it at the line which held the raft of logs to the boat and the gun was shouting along with the woodcutters' screaming.

A thousand logs were broken and bumping into each other and floating wildly in the fast rapids. The woodcutters tried to save them, but hundreds of logs were gone and lost.

The policeman, too, was gone the minute the raft was broken and the brother-in-law was so mad he took his axe and went after him, searching for him through the village.

Once, when I was with my husband in Kudangan, there was a boat from town that never arrived. It was overloaded with sacks of sugar for sale and when it sank, the sugar was gone along with the pasengers, sweetening the once lovely river. In the morning, one of the wives came to the river when we were washing and bathing, telling us with her mourning voice that her husband lost everything in the sunken boat, including some gold presents for her. Once again our mother river was angry with us. Our old people had to give offerings after the accident. There was not enough offering so the spirit of the river got angry with us.

In Topin Durai, the small rapids with big rocks down by the village, there was a small building where we kept the offerings and the chief of law was sowing yellow rice with *mantras* in the river to feed the spirit and asking protection for our village. Now, when I go back to the village, the Topin Durai is shallow and it's lost the whirlpool that once almost sucked me to my death. There are no fast rapids there any more, only a small, lazy stream with gravel. "It's gone by the flood," my aunty told me. They had many floods which carried dirt and soil from the head of the river, where there is all the timber cutting. It's destroyed the once lovely Delang, which was sometimes so friendly but which sometimes without warning would flow fiercely and destroy everything. Many people have thrown away their amulets for praying to their old god of the river, and although in the past there were always offerings hanging in the trees, now you have to search to find one and sometimes never see anything.

May, 1997 was the time when the war between the Dayak people and the Madurese people in West Kalimantan was very sensitive. None of us was talking about what was happening because it was dangerous and would make problems. My father told me a little but he would not say much at the time since Kudangan village is just on the border of West Kalimantan and he was worried.

But one day while we were still there, a Dayak man came from Sekombulan, the last village at the border, and told us about the war. "Many people are killed," he said, and one of my cousins mocked him as a coward because he was away from West Kalimantan, where he was born.

He also told us about the *mangkok merah*, or "Red Bowl," tradition for Dayaks. "They lift the Red Bowl," he told us. It means Dayak people are sending a message to other Dayaks, warning them about the danger that might come from outsiders. One of my friends told me that when the war and the killing took place in West Kalimantan, the Red Bowl was announced and if it had been sent to Kudangan it would move along the Delang River, Batangkawa River, Lamandau and Belantikan. And no one could stop the killing. People who are not Dayak will be hunted and no one could stop it. The man told us that the war started because people from another island came to make a living in the place of Dayak people. Taking everything they could. They came to cultivate the land, mine the ground and destroy the Dayak's sacred

233

places. They destroyed the sacred burial sites and created jealousy and hatred between people.

"Many people were killed," a friend of mine said. She was in West Kalimantan when the killing took place. "The Dayak warriors only take Madura men," she told me. "They can smell them and recognize them and they'll be taken as soon as they find them." She told me how they did it. I felt grateful because the war had not come to my village and because my friend wouldn't go back to her job with the timber company.

My uncle told us that the chief of law was going to make a little ceremony on the grave of Jajar Malahui, the founder and first chief of Kudangan village. With some assistants, he helped a chief of law from Sekombulan and Pak Ajung, the highest chief along the Delang River. They were already waiting when we entered the longhouse. They sat on the floor on the rattan mat. In front of them was a small jar, a young female chicken, a plate piled with rice on top of which were some tongang leaf bracelets. Another old plate was filled with the village's sacred amulets. The chief of law showed us a single deer horn. "It is very rare," he said and showed us some old stones of peculiar shape. The chief took out those amulets only on special occasions such as this one. Some of the men had not seen these amulets before.

A moment later the wife of the chief brought us each a glass of rice wine. Soon the chief of law from Sekombulan village started the ceremony, spelling some mantras and speaking the high old language we called god language. I picked up some words; he was asking for the safety of the village. He mentioned some gods identified by the places where they live, at the head of the river and at the mouth. He sowed some grain he picked up from the plate while muttering the mantras and holding the chicken while the Kudangan chief held the knife and cut a little skin on the chicken's head and a few drops of blood fell on the rice before he released the upset chicken at the rear of the room.

After the praying they all got up and went out of the house, carrying the bamboo offering and we followed them, walking about two hundred metres to the grave of the village founder. When we arrived, all the men were squatting on the ground and led by the chief they prayed, sowing some rice, and pouring a little rice wine in the four directions. Before we all got home, we stopped at the old graves of the previous chief of Kudangan and his family, graves typical of the Kaharingan faith.

We'd been in Kudangan for five days before we got in our hired car to ride back to Pangkalan Bun. Karina was begging me to stay longer but as our time was very limited, Uncle Dehes gave her one of his puppies and she finally gave up begging me.

Back in Pangkalan Bun I asked my sister what was happening, but she would not tell me anything. "You could put all of us in jail if the police ever heard," was what she said. The election was about to take place and anything we said could be taken wrong. I felt uneasy since my family live among the Muslim people. Meanwhile, the killing between Dayaks and Muslims was still taking place.

The Red Bowl contains some stuff such as feathers, rice and human blood to symbolize our strong spirit to fight to the end. It might come as far south as Pasir Panjang, where Mrs. Birute lives. My father told me that some people there were preparing themselves with weapons. It's an old tradition which functions as a mediator between all the Dayak tribes to warn each other about outsiders. It is never used in an internal war.

When my family left Kudangan village that first time, we paddled our small, no-engine boat for many days. There was no road yet connecting the villages, only a small path used by villagers looking for firewood or going to a ladang. The forest along the riverside was dense and untouched. Birds were passing our boat peacefully and monkeys were hanging on the trees. My papah and one of his friends, Kadir, a Dayak man from a nearby village, took the duty of paddling. The journey was tiring and slow and by the time we reached the big, main river of Lamandau, the current was so slow that my papah had to work extra hard to paddle the boat down to Pangkalan Bun where our brothers were waiting.

Now, we travelled on the logging road again, passing hundreds of fallen trees. They go deep in the jungle to the find the huge trees, cutting them with chainsaws and dragging them out on trailers. The logging road crisscrosses the forest. Every time I come up, I feel something lost. The forest. The green. Everywhere we see the forest open and the logs everywhere along the riverside. Brown and huge. We do not have our forest any more. Instead, Karina got out of the car and I saw her jumping from one log to another log where they were scattered on the ground. The road was bumpy and broken from the rain and the logging trailers which take thousands of logs away everyday.

The worst is, we can imagine the timber companies taking over everything and the goldmines digging the ground so that in the future the Dayak people will only watch the empty space with longing in their eyes, remembering that their grandparents once lived there surrounded by green, planting rice in the cleared field, hunting in the deep forest for deer and wild boar with a spear and a bunch of hunting dogs, making salt meat or smoking it under the longhouse, or making delicious pork cooked in a bamboo cylinder.

Such a life.

Their eyes will be full of longing for the evening party once held in the longhouse with rice wine and dancing, with joy filling the air.

Now the house is just a normal small house. No more party. No more dancing and what makes me most sad is that there will be no more longhouses. Sooner or later, young people will cut them down and replace them with city-like houses. The dragon door once standing as a pride of the owners is now replaced with plywood by their children, who prefer a modern-looking house. The longhouse will disappear and soon the dragon door will be only a story from mouth to mouth in our community. Our children will never know how it looked. No dragon carved door, just plywood.

We have hundreds of timber companies, big and small, roaming for wood and cutting thousands of trees once surrounding the Dayak villages. They build a base camp for cutting the wood with chainsaws, then send them down to the main camp on the river. The government says it is to supply the world's need for wood. In our town, only a couple of kilometres away there is a huge timber company that is a joint venture between Indonesians and Koreans. People say the main stockholder was our president's wife. They make plywood and send thousands of logs to the factory everyday. The factory works day and night and thick smoke comes up from the huge chimney, very dark. Those trees have been dragged out of the forest along the timber road which was cut from the heart of my village. No doubt many of them come from my village up the river and I wonder if some of them are the trees I used to climb on many years ago. There are some big fruit trees left in people's fruit gardens, but we can't expect to see ramin, meranti (mahagony), kruing, idat or ironwood any more. They have almost disappeared. We would have to go deep into the heart of the forest where some of the rare trees are left.

After my generation, my children or my grandchildren later on will never know there were many valuable trees surrounding our village before. They will never know what it is like to climb the big trees. They will never even know what they looked like. All they have left to see are small trees and bushes and the huge timber road winding from one village to another village, cutting through the place they are told was a forest long ago. Karina, my little daughter, will never know there was a forest by our village; she will only hear the story from her mother, how her mother went to the forest looking for wild fruit, collecting wild vegetables and the young shoots from the forest which were later served on the table. She will never know how dependent we were on the forest — her great-grandparents, her grandparents and her parents. She will never know the feeling of losing her roots, since the forest was our living place. Karina, your mother was born among the people of the Dayak Delang tribe in the place of the partridge and the wild buffalo. There, in Kudangan village, I spent eight years of my life. I never dreamed that it would change, that the longhouses that were once our pride would be cut down by the children who were born in them. I never knew that I would watch our culture disappearing, or that I would put my only hope in a book so that people who care about us will help us regain our old pride and regain our forest, our soul and living, our tribal land.

Oh Karina, I wish that I would be able to teach you so many things: how to find wild vegetables and how to recognize the plants for traditional medicine. Do you know your mother almost cut off her finger while collecting firewood? But she picked up the keladi plant (taro) and squeezed the sap on the cut and let the juice dry on it and the cut instantly closed and healed.

Karina, long ago your people went through a small trail in the forest to make a ladang. The wood was cut and the field cleared, then they left the wood to dry. They put a stick somewhere on the edge of the field to tell people that it was owned. When the wood dried, the farmer went back and burned the field to produce the ash to enrich the soil. The farmer would sow the rice and plant cassava or corn among the young shoots.

Now the path where they used to walk in the shade of the green forest is gone. You won't find it. You have the choice of walking on the timber road. Wide and hot. Hot and long. Your eyes will be tired from the big empty red road.

Once our people would leave the house and go to the ladang, planting rice or other things, then come back in the evening with a backpack full of vegetables and cassava leaves or fresh cucumber. They would make a delicious crushed cucumber mixed with baked fish paste and smoked river fish. They would have it with hot rice still fragrant from the new harvest. With all the family, they would sit together in front of the firestove, eating the boiled cassava leaves along with spicy sambal and talking about how many kulak they're going to have in the next harvest.

Then they would talk about where to plant the next ladang because they can't use the old one twice in a short time or the land will no longer be fertile. They might grow another plant in the old field. It could be rattan, rubber or fruit trees. And they'd leave it and let it grow by itself. If there were plants in the field nobody would dare take it over. It belonged to its first owner and he'd come back after a couple of years to collect the forest material he'd planted.

After a couple of years the soil would be rich once more and they might use it again for a ladang. There, in the same place, they'd make a small hut on the edge of the field and start to work again, cutting the wood with an axe, burning it and planting the field again with rice. Before the rice sprouts came up they'd hurry to plant some corn in between them, so before the harvest of rice he could harvest sweet corn.

What a pleasure to bake young corn next to the hut. The fragrance would fill the air. Tasty and sweet.

I wish that someday you'll see, too, how important the forest is, that life is started in the forest which gives us breath when we're born and finally when we die we are buried there.

For us, all these things had meaning.

Afterword

RISKA, with Linda Spalding's help, has produced a very readable book. Not only does she present her message in a lively and interesting manner, but she manages to express some of the conflicts and ambivalences — both personal and societal — confronting forest people around the world today. Her story, with its balanced portrayal of both men and women, manages to convey the realities of life as these women and men cope with their changing world.

Riska tells of the life experience of a young Dayak woman who moved from a remote area in Borneo to a city nearer the coast, and eventually to Bali. She skilfully weaves her recent experiences in the city with her memories of life in the village and in the forest. In this way, she successfully seduces readers, unfamiliar with life in Borneo, along an intimate path that introduces them to some of the wonders of life in that forest land.

Writing as a woman, her account contributes substantially both to our ongoing attempts to understand women's lives — recognizing the diversity encompassed therein — and to understand how women's life experiences and roles respond to changing circumstances.

WOMEN'S VOICES

The 1980s marked an explosion of interest in trying to understand women's lives. This interest manifested itself with formal "women in development" and "women's studies" programs. Research projects were initiated that looked at what women were doing and thinking, from an outsider's perspective. There were calls for disaggregation of statistics by gender, for greater involvement of professional women on research-and-development teams, and for greater attention to local women's needs and interests. Such research continues, gradually shifting from "women in development" to "gender and diversity" approaches that recognize a) the necessity to take both men's and women's lives into account, and b) the comparability between gender differences and other intra-cultural variations like ethnicity, caste, age, etc.

I recently completed a methodological test among the Dayak Iban and Melayu in West Kalimantan — indeed in the very area that Riska describes in her visits with her German friend (near Lanjak). Our approach followed the "outsider-initiated tradition." We tried to assess people's well-being in and around local timber concessions. We explicitly tried to assess women's well-being to the same degree as men's: we had equal numbers of women and men on our research teams; we almost succeeded in getting equal numbers of male and female respondents to questions about voice in forest management; we designed one method to address men's and women's perceptions of gender roles in natural resource management; and we used qualitative techniques to assess women's access to resources over time (Colfer et al. 1997). Yet, we came away still dissatisfied with our access to women's perspectives, interests and conditions.

In some of these external approaches, researchers objectify women, portraying them (us) within the framework of one dominant paradigm or another, thus (albeit unintentionally) reinforcing the legitimacy of systems of knowledge and perhaps oppression that feminists and others decry. Too little seems to change, particularly for Third World women, as a result of these efforts.

It may be that women's lives are inherently more difficult to capture than men's. Ardener (1975) provided a convincing compendium of articles showing how women's knowledge is "muted." I have argued elsewhere that women and other muted groups have to deal with more complex realities than do dominant groups (1983), which would imply that depicting their overall reality would be concomitantly more complex. Bateson (1990) has written of Western women "composing" their lives — suggesting a malleability that could also be difficult to capture. On the other hand, we may simply be hampered by conceptual tools created by a male-dominated world that has only recently begun to recognize women as worthy of attention.

Riska: Memories of a Dayak Girlhood is part of an increasingly popular genre in which local women tell their own tales, autobiographically (e.g., Barnes and Boddy 1994; Townsend 1995), or by means of extensive quotations (e.g., Tsing 1993), in an attempt to resolve this problem of satisfactorily reflecting or representing women's lives. An autobiography gives an in-depth portrayal of one life, with both its idiosyncrasies and its reflection of the culture or lifeway from which the individual comes — all from the insider's perspective. *Riska*, to my knowledge, represents the first such published account of a Dayak woman's life.

ETHNOGRAPHY OF DAYAK WOMEN

But why are we particularly interested to know about a Dayak woman's life? One of the most compelling reasons in my mind is that traditionally Dayaks have represented societies characterized by the closest thing to gender equity in the world. Let me hasten to add that Dayaks have not exhibited perfect gender equality — only *comparative* equity (see Sutlive's 1993 compendium). Still, that this is so represents an important human accomplishment, something about which feminists and others concerned to enhance equity in the world may want to know more.

My first encounter with Dayaks came in 1979, when I moved in with the Kenyah family of a resettlement village headman, in Long Segar, and began a year-long research project (which was, to a degree, to become a lifelong research project) on "Interactions between People and Forests in East Kaliman-tan." Having done research on gender issues in an American log-ging community and briefly in Iran, I was tuned in to women's issues. I was immediately struck by Kenyah women's autonomy in daily life, their voice in family and community decision-making, and the respect granted them by others (discussed in

Colfer 1985a,b). I gradually learned of their important role in subsistence — something Sanday (1974) has shown to be a necessary, if not sufficient, prerequisite for high female status.

But as my time in the community lengthened, and I made a brief visit to their remote home village of Long Ampung (in the very centre of Borneo), I began to realize that there were not-so-subtle pressures at work in Long Segar that had the potential to adversely affect the high status with which I was so impressed:

Wage-labour opportunities were increasingly available to men (not women), and becoming more important as more and more desired commodities were only available with money. Local wage opportunities were primarily in the timber industry, one of the few remaining professions where men's greater physical strength is important. Women were also disadvantaged in wage-labour opportunities by the need to bear, nurse and care for children;

New technological devices like chainsaws were making women less important in land clearing. Men found that they could now clear ten times as much land in a day as they had been able to do with axes and bush knives; the only partially comparable new efficiency in female-dominated phases of the rice production process was the rice-huller. Similarly the weight of outboard motors removed women's self-sufficiency in transport. Most women needed men's help to carry the engines down the river-bank in the morning and back up to the safety of the house each night;

Negative stereotypes of Dayaks in general, but particularly Dayak women, by more dominant ethnic groups who were beginning to move into the area, eroded self-confidence. Dayaks were considered "primitive;" many other Indonesians believed Dayaks had tails; and Dayak women were considered to be promiscuous; the expectation by these same groups that men were the "rice-winners," and women homebodies was reinforced nationally and religiously in several contexts (see Tsing 1993 for many examples of this kind of process);

Agricultural extension programs were directed solely at men, despite Dayak women's traditional dominance in agriculture; etc.

Accepting Sanday's conclusion about the importance of women's productive involvement for their status, I did an analysis of women's 1979-80 involvement in rice production in Long Ampung (representing a "traditional" setting) and in the resettlement village of Long Segar (a village in transition, or, possibly on a "slippery slope" with regard to gender equity). The findings (Colfer 1991) confirmed my fears. In Long Segar, rice production was positively correlated with the number of agriculturally active men in the family; whereas in Long Ampung the reverse was true. Men's involvement in agriculture was expanding at the expense of women's in Long Segar, the village being bombarded with national propaganda about women as homemakers. In Long Ampung, women remained the mainstay of rice production. This finding was further strengthened when we collected and analyzed data from 1980 to 1990 (Colfer with Dudley 1993). The sex ratio of adults actively involved in rice production went from 0.87 in 1980 (women dominant) to 1.27 in 1990 (men dominant). This was contrasted to five years of data in the still remote Long Ampung, where the mean for 1985-1990 was still 0.81.

DAYAK WOMEN IN THE CITY: RISKA'S ACCOUNT

These studies, however, all focused on the situation of women in the village. Riska, in contrast, focuses attention on what happens to a Dayak woman when she leaves the village. I know young Kenyah women who have left the village and experienced ambivalence, violence and difficulties back home, similar to those described by Riska. Her situation is not unique. What is unique is having an account, in her own words, of her life story.

As she tells her story, we can imagine the interplay between the *comparatively* benign male-female relations of the Dayaks on the one hand, and the dominant, more male-dominated, wider society on the other. As Dayak women interact with members of the dominant culture, it is not unusual for their self-confidence to suffer, confronted repeatedly by both gender and ethnic insensitivity and prejudice. Tsing (1993) writes of a similar situation between Central Kalimantan's Meratus Dayaks and Muslim Banjars. Interestingly, Tsing (1993) also tells women's stories of alien romance—of love affairs with men from other ethnic groups—quite comparable to some of Riska's experiences.

Riska's references to "helping" her husband or her father in agricultural pursuits reflects the impacts that the views of the wider society have had on her own perceptions — impacts one could expect to be more noticeable in a family with a teacher for a mother. Her mother, during the course of formal education, was exposed longer to the dominant society's views and, busy with teaching, was probably not available for much agricultural labour herself.

Riska has dramatically and skilfully captured disturbing trends in Dayak societies. She is able to weave images of her childhood in the village into and throughout her current city life. The difficult choices that people must now make, confronted as they are with the draw of modern life, are presented in counterpoint with the fears, beauties, realities of traditional Dayak culture. Riska has experienced both a traditional Dayak life and the dangers and delights of "modern" life in Indonesia's cities. Her story is a forerunner of what the young women of today and tomorrow may face.

Most Indonesians are Muslim, with Islamic views of appropriate women's behaviour (albeit considerably gentler versions than one finds in the Middle East). Dayak women — Christian or animist — have a reputation, among many other ethnic groups, for being "fast." This perception may in part be a reflection of the fact that much more open communication between the sexes is normal among Dayak groups. The trust among Dayaks who have grown up together cannot safely be extended to men coming in from the outside. Among the Kenyah and Iban Dayak, for instance, there was a tradition of young men and women lying together before marriage (theoretically, and apparently frequently, without sexual congress), as part of the normal courting pattern. Among the Kenyah, this practice — though disapproved of by missionaries — was viewed very much like dating is in the US; I saw many parallels between Dayak and American courting patterns — in marked distinction from that approved by other Indonesian ethnic groups.

CULTURAL DIVERSITY

Women have been the focus of this discussion so far. Yet that bundle of features we refer to as "the Dayak way of life" contains a number of more general features that seem worthy of note. Women's roles, as the primary enculturators of the young, are significant also in maintaining the characteristics listed below, characteristics that drew me to Dayak life and have tied me to it ever since:

Their sense of humour and equanimity in the face of life's recurring disasters (floods, pest invasions, accidents, death). A simple, but representative, example that has stayed with me: I watched a group of men floating a log raft down the Kayan River in Long Ampung in 1980. Somehow the logs came untied and the raft began to come apart. In these circumstances, I remember thinking, American men would have been angry and yelling at each other; these Kenyah men were laughing as they set about correcting the problem.

Their generosity. I genuinely thought I was a generous person until I went to live with the Kenyah. Having more than one needs and *not* sharing it is one of the most heinous "sins" that a person can commit. I remember people's horror and disapproval when I refused to make my eleven-year-old daughter share the myriad small Barbie doll accoutrements with which she had filled the single suitcase she was able to bring with her so far from her home. The Kenyah both ask from and give freely to each other. Kaskija (1995) interprets this characteristic among the related Punan less positively, calling it "demand sharing."

Their recognition of differing strengths. My near neighbours were an extended family, composed of two old brothers married to two old sisters (a pattern considered taboo before they became Christian), with two married children and their families. This group overtly recognized and praised each other's strengths, drawing on them as needed. One man was a good hunter; another a good fisher; both women were excellent rice farmers; an old man, besides being revered for his abilities in the forest, was a good weaver of baskets and fish traps. The cooking skills of both husband and wife in one nuclear family were recognized as outstanding. Approval follows from individual strengths, far more than gender stereotypes.

The acceptance of responsibility for each other's well-being. As the Kenyah will point out to you, in serious discussion, there are no Kenyah sleeping under bridges, abandoned by loved ones (as one sees in Java). Although in daily life people are responsible for themselves and their families, in hard times family and friends chip in to help. Not to do so would be unthinkable — partly of course because you may, yourself, be in need one day (cf. Dove's, 1988).

The value placed on hard work, initiative and creativity. An important criterion for spouse selection is a demonstrated propensity for these traits. Potential spouses are commented on, with regard to their diligence, intelligence and abilities; children are steered (though not forced) towards other young people who manifest these traits. And young people are very busy demonstrating them to the community.

It goes without saying that Dayaks — as human beings — differ among groups, and individuals differ markedly within groups. Yet their ways of life are tied by common threads of value. They represent part of the global treasure trove of cultures; and they represent a kind of insurance against the failure of the currently dominant, Western lifestyle, a failure that is not so difficult to envision.

Riska ends her narrative with an address to her daughter, reflecting her regret that Karina will not have the forest-based memories that have enriched her own life. Knowing the people of Borneo as I do, and indeed having my own precious forest-based memories, I share her feeling.

Riska's own life has been a journey from the semi-traditional to the semi-modern. Her parents' "mixed marriage," her early residence in a forest community her mother considered "beneath them," and her mother's relatively high educational level, all conspired to deny Riska the firm emotional base in village life that many Dayaks have. In a sense, she could never have fully enjoyed village life, as she felt her father did. Yet she had enough of a feeling for its meaning and its pleasures to realize what she was missing.

Her "high class" rural upbringing could hardly have prepared her for the prejudice and disdain she (and any Dayak) would encounter from urban Muslims. Her father's inability to cope financially with urban life — despite her mother's "respectable" position — clinched her classification, with other Dayaks, at the bottom of the social heap. Her ability to accomplish what she has is a reflection of her true intelligence and an unusual drive.

I met Riska (and Linda Spalding) in 1997, when I had read an early draft of Riska's manuscript. We discussed the questions I had from an ethnographic perspective. What I remember best about Riska was her quiet self-confidence. She exudes a calmness that is not unusual among village Dayaks — but *is* unusual among those who have tried to adjust to city life. Meeting her renewed my hope that a solution can be found that will retain some of the admirable and desirable aspects of Dayak lifeways while granting Dayaks access to those aspects of "modern" life that they want. I have faith in her ability — despite the problems she recounts in her story — to cope creatively with the life she has ahead of her. The degree to which her daughter will retain those admirable Dayak traits is what remains in question.

My own life has been infinitely enriched by my involvement with the indigenous peoples of Borneo. They have opened up to me vistas of human possibility that I did not know existed. There is no way to repay them. But perhaps we can contribute to a global atmosphere that will allow them to continue and to develop along their own paths — preferably maintaining their link to the beautiful forests of Borneo. Perhaps *Riska: Memories of a Dayak Girlhood* can give readers a taste of these people's lives, alert us all to the dangers confronting forest people as they try to come to terms with a wider world, and perhaps even help to create a nurturing, accepting setting where they can thrive.

Carol J. Pierce Colfer
Bogor, Indonesia, *1999*

Bibliography

Ardener, Shirley, ed. *Perceiving Women.* London: Malaby Press, 1975

Barnes, Virginia Lee and Janice Boddy. *Aman: The Story of a Somali Girl.* Toronto: Knopf Canada, 1994.

Bateson, Mary Catherine. *Composing a Life.* New York: Plume Publishing, 1990.

Colfer, Carol J. Pierce. "Female Status and Action in Two Dayak Communities." In *Women in Asia and the Pacific: Towards an East-West*

Dialogue, edited by M. Goodman. Honolulu: University of Hawaii Press, 1985.

_____ "On Circular Migration: From the Distaff Side." *Labour Circulation and the Labour Process*, edited by G. Standing. Geneva: Croom Helm Ltd., 1985.

_____ "On Communication Among 'Unequals.'" *International Journal of Intercultural Communication* 7:263-283, 1983.

_____ "Indigenous Rice Production and the Subtleties of Culture Change." *Agriculture and Human Values* VIII(1,2):67-84, 1991.

Colfer, Carol J. Pierce and Richard G. Dudley. *Shifting Cultivation in Indonesia: Marauders or Managers of the Forest?* Rome: FAO Community Forestry Case No. 6, 1993.

Colfer, Carol J. Pierce, Reed L. Wadley, Joseph Woelfel and Emily Harwell. "Heartwood to Bark: Gender Issues in Sustainable Forest Management." *Women in Natural Resources* 18(4):7-14, 1997.

Dove, Michael. "The ecology of intoxication among the Kantu of West Kalimantan." In *The real and imagined role of culture in development: Case studies from Indonesia*, edited by Michael Dove. Honolulu: University of Hawaii Press, 1988: 139-182.

Karskija, Lars. *Punan Malinau: the persistence of an unstable culture.* Doctoral dissertation, Uppsala University, Sweden, 1995.

Sanday, Peggy. "Female status in the public domain." In *Women, Culture and Society*, edited by Michelle Z. Rosaldo and Louise Lamphere. Stanford: Stanford University Press, 1974: 189-206.

Sutlive, Vinson, ed. *Male and Female in Borneo*. Shanghai, VA: Borneo Research Council Monograph Series, 1993.

Townsend, Janet Gabriel. *Women's Voices from the Rainforest*. London: Routledge, 1995.

Tsing, Anna Lowenhaupt. *In the Realm of the Diamond Queen*. Princeton: Princeton University Press, 1993.

Riska Orpa Sari, 30, was born in the Dayak village of Kudangan, on the banks of a remote river in Kalimantan, Borneo. She speaks two Dayak dialects, Indonesian and English, and has trained and worked as a forest guide.

Linda Spalding is a Canadian novelist and editor of *Brick, A Literary Journal*. She met Riska in Borneo while doing research for her acclaimed work of non-fiction, *A Dark Place in the Jungle*.

Carol J. Pierce Colfer is an anthropologist with a particular interest in forest cultures. She lives in Indonesia, where she works for the Center for International Forestry Research, based in Bogor.